P9-AEY-882

KF4750 .N29 1998
Nardo, Don,
The Bill of Rights /
Northeast Lakeview Colleg
33784000123703

Northeast Lakeview College

33784 0001 2370 3

The Bill of Rights

[OPPOSING VIEWPOINTS® DIGESTS]

The Bill of Rights

DON NARDO

$$\left[\begin{array}{c} \textbf{OPPOSING} \\ \textbf{VIEWPOINTS}^{\textregistered} \\ \text{DIGESTS} \end{array}\right]$$

Greenhaven Press Inc., San Diego, California

No part of this book may be reproduced or used in any form or by any means, electrical, mechanical, or otherwise, including, but not limited to, photocopy, recording, or any information storage and retrieval system, without prior written permission from the publisher.

Every effort has been made to trace owners of copyrighted material.

Library of Congress Cataloging-in-Publication Data

Nardo, Don, 1947–
    The Bill of Rights / Don Nardo.
       p.   cm. — (Opposing viewpoints digests)
    Includes bibliographical references and index.
    Summary: Includes an overview of the original debate over the need for a bill of rights, an exploration of some later debates about rights issues, and an appendix of original documents.
    ISBN 1-56510-741-1 (lib. ed : alk. paper). — ISBN 1-56510-740-3 (pbk. : alk. paper)
    1. Civil rights—United States—Juvenile literature. 2. United States. Constitution. 1st–10th Amendments—Juvenile literature. [1. Civil rights. 2. United States. Constitution. 1st–10th Amendments.]   I. Title. II. Series.
KF4750.N29   1998
342.73'085—dc21   97-27519
                                                        CIP

Cover Photo: Library of Congress
Library of Congress, 11, 18, 30, 84, 89
National Archives, 34, 95
North Wind Picture Archives, 12
From the Collection of the Supreme Court, 67

©1998 by Greenhaven Press, Inc.
PO Box 289009, San Diego, CA 92198-9009

Printed in the U.S.A.

CONTENTS

FOREWORD

"The only way in which a human being can make some approach to knowing the whole of a subject is by hearing what can be said about it by persons of every variety of opinion and studying all modes in which it can be looked at by every character of mind. No wise man ever acquired his wisdom in any mode but this."
—John Stuart Mill

Greenhaven Press's Opposing Viewpoints Digests in history are designed to aid in examining important historical issues in a way that develops critical thinking and evaluating skills. Each book presents thought-provoking argument and stimulating debate on a single topic. In analyzing issues through opposing views, students gain a social and historical context that cannot be discovered in textbooks. Excerpts from primary sources reveal the personal, political, and economic side of historical topics such as the American Revolution, the Great Depression, and the Bill of Rights. Students begin to understand that history is not a dry recounting of facts, but a record founded on ideas—ideas that become manifest through lively discussion and debate. Digests immerse students in contemporary discussions: Why did many colonists oppose a bill of rights? What was the original intent of the New Deal and on what grounds was it criticized? These arguments provide a foundation for students to assess today's debates on censorship, welfare, and other issues. For example, *The Great Depression: Opposing Viewpoints Digests* offers opposing arguments on controversial issues of the time as well as views and interpretations that interest modern historians. A major debate during Franklin D. Roosevelt's administration was whether the president's New Deal programs would lead to a permanent welfare state, creating a citizenry dependent on government money. *The Great Depression* covers this issue from both historical and modern perspectives, allowing students to critically evaluate arguments both in the context of their time and through the benefit of historical hindsight.

This emphasis on debate makes Digests a useful tool for writing reports, research papers, and persuasive essays. In addition to supplying students with a range of possible topics and supporting material, the Opposing Viewpoints Digests offer unique features through which young readers acquire and sharpen critical thinking and reading skills. To assure an appropriate and consistent reading level for young adults, all essays in each volume are written by a single author. Each essay heavily quotes readable primary sources that are fully cited to allow for further research and documentation. Thus, primary sources are introduced in a context to enhance comprehension.

In addition, each volume includes extensive research tools, including a section comprising excerpts from original documents pertaining to the issue under discussion. In *The Bill of Rights*, for example, readers can examine the English Magna Carta, the Virginia State Bill of Rights drawn up in 1776, and various opinions by U.S. Supreme Court justices in key civil rights cases, as well as an unabridged version of the U.S. Bill of Rights. These documents both complement the text and give students access to a wide variety of relevant sources in a single volume. Additionally, a "facts about" section allows students to peruse facts and statistics that pertain to the topic. These statistics are also fully cited, allowing students to question and analyze the credibility of the source. Two bibliographies, one for young adults and one listing the author's sources, are also included; both are annotated to guide student research. Finally, a comprehensive index allows students to scan and locate content efficiently.

Greenhaven's Opposing Viewpoints Digests, like Greenhaven's higher level and critically acclaimed Opposing Viewpoints Series, have been developed around the concept that an awareness and appreciation for the complexity of seemingly simple issues is particularly important in a democratic society. In a democracy, the common good is often, and very appropriately, decided by open debate of widely varying views. As one of democracy's greatest advocates, Thomas Jefferson, observed, "Difference of opinion leads to inquiry, and inquiry to truth." It is to this principle that Opposing Viewpoints Digests are dedicated.

"Give Great Quiet to the People": The Creation of the Bill of Rights

When the U.S. founding fathers drafted the original federal Constitution in 1787, they did not include a bill of rights, a list of fundamental freedoms guaranteed to all citizens. This seems quite strange and surprising to many people today; for in the more than two centuries since the ten articles of the U.S. Bill of Rights were ratified and accepted (December 15, 1791), most Americans have come to view these brief statements of basic rights, more or less, *as* the Constitution. As noted political scholar Eugene Hickok puts it:

> Ask any citizen where he can find in the Constitution provisions outlining the powers of the president, or the Congress, or the federal courts, and more often than not you will confront a blank stare. But it seems almost everyone is willing to assert that he or she enjoys freedom of speech, the virtues of separation between church and state, the right to bear arms, and the right to be protected against unreasonable searches and seizures. It's all right there in the Constitution.[1]

Actually, these and other similar protections are "right there" in the Bill of Rights, made up of the Constitution's first ten amendments. The story of how these amendments were conceived, debated, and eventually accepted is one of the most dramatic and interesting episodes in American history and

9

stands as a monument to both the democratic process and the memory of a handful of talented, passionate men.

The Weak and Inefficient Articles

Fifty-five delegates representing twelve of the thirteen original states convened the Federal Constitutional Convention in Philadelphia on May 14, 1787.[2] At that moment the infant nation had been governed for just over six years by the Articles of Confederation, a governmental document that had proved weak and ineffective in a number of ways. First, it did not provide for a chief executive, or president, to carry out public policies formulated by Congress; instead, various committees, panels, and individuals had to carry them out, an unnecessarily complicated, disorderly, and time-consuming process. Under the Articles, no law made by Congress was binding on a person unless his or her home state chose to enforce it. Moreover, Congress lacked the authority to tax and had to request contributions from the states, which were often unwilling to comply with such requests. Not surprisingly, the federal government eventually became nearly bankrupt.

In retrospect, another serious weakness of the Articles of Confederation was that it lacked a bill of rights. At the time, however, most leading American legislators did not see this as a problem, mainly because most states had drafted their own individual bills listing basic civil rights. The first of the original colonies to do so was Virginia, on June 12, 1776. The principal author of the Virginia Declaration of Rights was George Mason, a local planter who had became a skilled and popular legislator. Among the document's sixteen articles were several that, somewhat reworded, would later end up in the national Bill of Rights, including these provisions for due process of law and freedom of speech and religion:

> 8. That in all capital or criminal prosecutions a man hath a right to demand the cause and nature of his accusation, to be confronted with the accusers and

The U.S. founding fathers convene at the Federal Constitutional Convention at Independence Hall in Philadelphia.

witnesses, to call for evidence in his favor, and to a speedy trial by an impartial jury. . . .

12. That the freedom of the press is one of the great bulwarks of liberty, and can never be restrained. . . .

16. That religion . . . can be directed only by reason and conviction, not by force or violence; and therefore all men are equally entitled to the free exercise of religion.[3]

Earlier Civil Rights Declarations

These were not new ideas. Precedents for civil liberties already existed in English law traditions stretching back more than five hundred years, beginning with the signing of the Magna Carta, or "great charter," by King John in the year 1215. When King John decided to impose some unusually heavy taxes, the lords of his realm rejected the move. They

Rebellious barons force King John to sign the Magna Carta, one of the documents drafted to limit the power of English kings and safeguard religious and civil rights.

were used to paying only certain customary taxes and claimed that the king was exceeding his authority under the fair and natural "law of the land," which bound him as well as them. They forced him to sign the charter granting certain inalienable rights, among the provisions:

1. That the English Church shall be free, and shall
have her whole rights and her liberties inviolable. . . .
39. No free man shall be seized, or imprisoned, or
dispossessed . . . excepting by the legal judgment of
his peers, or by the laws of the land. . . .
40. To none will we sell [or] deny [or] delay right or
justice. . . .
63. That the men in our kingdom have
and hold the aforesaid liberties . . . full and entirely,
to them and their heirs.[4]

After the concessions made by the crown in the Magna Carta,
English kings required the consent of a council of their sub-
jects before enacting changes that affected the whole realm.
Over the next few centuries, that council developed into
Parliament, England's great bicameral legislature.

By the 1600s, Parliament had grown strong enough to challenge the monarchy for control of the government; and growing tensions led to a bloody civil war in the 1640s between the
supporters of the king and those of Parliament. Parliament
won and had the king beheaded, serving notice that the
monarchy must thereafter obey the country's accumulated
laws, which could only be changed by the legislature. The cul-
mination of Parliament's rise to supremacy was the 1689
English Bill of Rights, the most far-reaching declaration of
human rights up to that time and a direct precursor to the
later American version. Among other things, the English Bill
provided:

5. That it is the right of the subjects to petition the
King. . . .
9. That the freedom of speech, and debates or proceedings in Parliament, ought not to be impeached or
questioned. . . .
10. That excessive bail ought not to be required, nor
excessive fines imposed; nor cruel and unusual punishments inflicted.[5]

The authors of Virginia's bill of rights and similar bills in other colonies had also drawn on the ideas of popular and, at the time, somewhat controversial English and French political philosophers. One of the most influential of these was the seventeenth-century English writer John Locke. He advocated that human beings have certain God-given rights, among them life, liberty, and property, stating, for instance, that "the supreme power [of the state] cannot take from any man any part of his property without his own consent. For the preservation of property . . . [is] the end of government, and that for which men enter into society."[6] Further, Locke states, when rulers threaten or violate such rights, the people have the right to replace those rulers.

Jefferson Draws on Locke

Locke's ideas influenced all of the American founders, including Thomas Jefferson, author of another pivotal human rights statement, the Declaration of Independence. Jefferson drew freely on Locke in such now immortal phrases as "We hold these truths to be self-evident, that all men are created equal, that they are endowed by their Creator with certain unalienable Rights, that among these are Life, Liberty and the pursuit of Happiness"; and "Whenever any Form of Government becomes destructive of these ends, it is the Right of the People to alter or to abolish it, and to institute new Government."

Thus, in devising their individual bills of rights in the late 1770s, the American states had a long tradition of English civil rights and liberal political writings to draw on. The Americans, after all, had not rebelled against the mother country because it lacked government-backed freedoms; rather, the revolution had grown out of protests against specific British abuses of its American colonies. "The irony of the American revolution," political scholars Milton Cummings and David Wise point out, "is that the colonists, for the most part, rebelled because they felt they were being deprived of their rights as *Englishmen*."[7]

An Emotionally Wrenching Process

In the minds of most American leaders, the Declaration of Independence, the subsequent Revolutionary War, and the creation of state constitutions and bills of rights had restored those "deprived" rights. So, when the delegates met in Philadelphia in May 1787, they were worried less about basic rights and more about constructing a strong, flexible, workable governmental apparatus to run the country. Their mission, as they initially viewed it, was to amend and strengthen the existing Articles of Confederation; however, in the four months the convention lasted, they ended up creating a substantially new and much stronger Constitution and federal government.

Toward the end of the convention, some of the delegates voiced their concerns that the document, like its predecessor, the Articles, lacked a list of guaranteed personal liberties. This was especially troublesome, they said, because the new federal government was very powerful and might unfairly impose its will on both states and individuals. Responding to these concerns, on September 12 George Mason proposed that a list of guaranteed rights be added to the Constitution. He said he wished that "the plan [what the delegates called the incomplete Constitution at this time] had been prefaced with a bill of rights. It would give great quiet to the people."[8] Elbridge Gerry of Massachusetts agreed and moved for the preparation of such a bill. Mason quickly seconded him. But Connecticut's Roger Sherman argued that the bills of rights already created in a majority of the states were sufficient to guarantee civil rights; agreeing with this view, the states speedily voted unanimously not to create a federal bill of rights. For this reason, Mason, along with Gerry and Virginia's Edmund Randolph, refused to sign the finished Constitution.

The document then went to the state legislatures for ratification, which turned out to be a long and emotionally wrenching process.[9] In the months that followed, it became evident that Mason and others had a number of problems with the new Constitution, and they voiced their misgivings in their respective legislatures, in newspapers and pamphlets, and in public speeches. In the loud, spirited, and sometimes angry debate over ratification, those opposed, who demanded changes in the Constitution, became known as the Anti-Federalists; while those who wanted to accept the Constitution as it had been drafted were called the Federalists. The Anti-Federalists feared that the new government had too much power, that the office of president might grow into a new kingship, and that the Congress, as outlined in the Constitution, would not truly represent all the people.

But the Anti-Federalists' biggest complaint, and the one that resonated most with average citizens, was the Constitution's lack of a bill of rights. Mason spoke for many when he said:

> There is no declaration of rights: and the laws of the general government being paramount to the laws and constitutions of the several states, the declarations of rights, in the separate states, are no security. Nor are the people secured even in the enjoyment of the benefit of the common law, which stands here upon no other foundation than its having been adapted by the respective acts forming the constitutions of the several states. . . . The Congress may [if the current Constitution is enacted] grant monopolies in trade and commerce, constitute new crimes, inflict unusual and severe punishments, and extend their power as far as they shall think proper; so that the state legislatures have no security for the powers now presumed to remain to them; or the people for their rights. There is no declaration of any kind for preserving the liberty of the press, the trial by jury in civil cases, nor against the danger of standing armies in time of peace.[10]

New York's Alexander Hamilton, a staunch and leading Federalist, responded that bills of rights were usually just lists of aphorisms, or declarations of principles, that served to draw a line between the powers of a ruler and the rights of his subjects; such declarations are unnecessary, he said, when the people rule themselves. Moreover, a bill of rights might even be dangerous. "It has been several times truly remarked," he stated,

> that bills of rights are in their origin, stipulations between kings and their subjects . . . reservations of rights not surrendered to the prince. Such was the Magna Charta, obtained by the [English] Barons, sword in hand, from King John. . . . Such also was the . . . act of Parliament, called the [English] Bill of Rights. It is evident, therefore, that . . . they have no application to constitutions professedly founded upon the power of the people. . . . Here [in the phrase "We the people of the United States," which opens the Constitution] is a better recognition of popular rights than volumes of those aphorisms which make the principal figure in several of our state bills of rights, and which would sound much better in a treatise of ethics than in a constitution of government. . . . I go further and affirm that bills of rights . . . are not only unnecessary in the proposed constitution, but would even be dangerous. They would contain various exceptions to powers which are not granted [to the government]; and on this very account, would afford a . . . pretext to claim more than were granted. For why declare that things shall not be done which there is no power to do? Why for instance, should it be said, that the liberty of the press shall not be restrained, when no power is given by which restrictions may be imposed?[11]

Madison Changes His Mind

Virginia's James Madison, one of the principal authors of the Constitution drafted in Philadelphia, was at first a Federalist.

Like Hamilton, he concluded that the manner in which the Constitution divided power between the federal and state governments and also among the three federal branches (executive, legislative, and judicial) was enough of a safeguard against tyranny. Therefore, a bill of rights was unnecessary.

James Madison initially opposed adding a bill of rights to the Constitution but was later persuaded by colleagues to support the Anti-Federalists' desire for a rights declaration.

But as the debate progressed, Madison began to waver. First, his highly influential colleagues, Thomas Jefferson and John Adams, both came out in favor of a rights declaration. Second, it became increasingly apparent that Madison's political career, most immediately his role in the new Congress that would convene when (and if) the Constitution was ratified, might be threatened if he did not change his mind. His fellow Virginian, Patrick Henry, a fervent Anti-Federalist, made sure that he was not chosen as a senator to the new Congress.[12] When Madison then sought a seat in the House of Representatives, Henry, knowing the other man hated campaigning, persuaded Madison's friend, James Monroe, to run against him.

In addition to these motivations for giving in to the Anti-Federalists, Madison reasoned correctly that backing a bill of rights would be a step toward compromise, an effective way of gaining his opponents' support for the Constitution. After a few months, therefore, he stated that he now felt a bill of rights would satisfy "the minds of well-meaning opponents, and [provide] additional [safe]guards in favor of liberty." Further, he said:

> It is my sincere opinion that the Constitution ought to be revised and that the first Congress meeting under it, ought to prepare and recommend to the States for ratification, the most satisfactory provisions for all essential rights, particularly the rights of Conscience in the fullest latitude, the freedom of the press, trials by jury, security against general warrants, etc.[13]

This sort of compromise both satisfied the Anti-Federalists and ensured the Constitution's ratification. Mason, Henry, and their supporters agreed to ratify the document on the condition that Madison and the other Federalists pledged to add a bill of rights afterward. Beginning with Massachusetts, which ratified in February 1788, most states that followed suit submitted proposed articles for a rights declaration. In all,

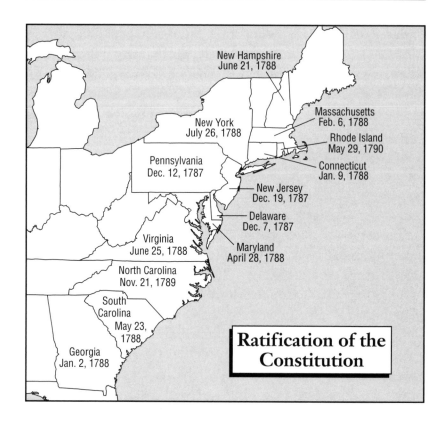

New Hampshire
June 21, 1788

Massachusetts
Feb. 6, 1788

New York
July 26, 1788

Rhode Island
May 29, 1790

Pennsylvania
Dec. 12, 1787

Connecticut
Jan. 9, 1788

New Jersey
Dec. 19, 1787

Delaware
Dec. 7, 1787

Virginia
June 25, 1788

Maryland
April 28, 1788

North Carolina
Nov. 21, 1789

South
Carolina
May 23,
1788

Georgia
Jan. 2, 1788

Ratification of the Constitution

more than two hundred such amendments were suggested, and these became the raw material for the process of creating a federal bill of rights that Congress undertook in the summer of 1789.

The Drafting and Ratification Processes

True to his word, Madison, on taking his seat in the first session of the House of Representatives, assumed a leadership role in that process, approaching the task of amending the Constitution with diligence and vigor. Originally, he wanted to incorporate the changes into the text of the document rather than adding a list of amendments at its end. Among his proposed revisions, drawn substantially from the Virginia Declaration of Rights, was the addition of the statements: "No person shall be subject, except in cases of impeachment, to more than one punishment or one trial for the same offense; nor shall be compelled to be a witness against himself"; and "No State shall violate the equal rights of conscience, or the freedom of the press, or trial by jury in criminal cases."[14]

Although Madison's colleagues decided to leave the main body of the Constitution intact and append the rights amendments at the end, Madison's rights proposals were highly influential to the process. With some combining of separate articles and minor rewording of these and others, most of his proposals ended up in the final product; a notable exception was an allowance for the right of conscientious objectors to hire substitutes to take their place in battle: "No person religiously scrupulous of bearing arms shall be compelled to render military service in person."[15]

In contrast with the earlier heated debates about the need for a bill of rights, the drafting process went relatively smoothly. This was because all of the congressmen and senators shared the rich British legal and political tradition that had produced the English Bill of Rights and the writings of John Locke; and so, most had similar ideas about what constituted civil rights. "By the time the members of the First Congress got down to the business of drafting the amendments," Hickok explains,

> a general consensus existed regarding just what sorts of things should be included in a bill of rights. And there was general agreement over what was meant by such ideas as freedom of speech and of the press and the right to bear arms. There was a need to refine the terms and clarify their meaning. . . . But for the most part, the deliberations demonstrate remarkable consensus, especially when compared with the sort of controversy that typically surrounds contemporary debate over similar issues.[16]

Thus, after some consolidation and rewording of the proposed amendments, the House, by the two-thirds majority needed, fairly speedily adopted a preliminary list and passed it on to the Senate. There, some changes in format and more rewording took place. Finally, the proposals went to a conference committee made up of members of both houses; and, after still more rewording, a list of twelve final amendments emerged. On September 25, 1789, Congress sent this list to the states for ratification.

The ratification process also proved largely smooth and uncontroversial. The first two amendments, dealing with congressional appointment and compensation, were summarily rejected; but the remaining ten, after being renumbered, proved satisfactory to all the state legislatures. During the ratification process, Vermont entered the Union (March 4, 1791), which meant that eleven states had to ratify the bill before it became law. Perhaps it was poetic justice that Virginia, home of Mason and Madison, widely seen as the fathers of the bill, became the eleventh and pivotal state to ratify. When Virginia accepted it on December 15, 1791, the final version of the Bill of Rights officially became part of the U.S. Constitution.[17]

Soon after this historic day, Mason—whose prediction that passing a bill of rights would "give great quiet to the people" came true—retired from public life. Suffering from ill health, he died on October 7, 1792, at the age of sixty-seven. The much younger Madison went on to become secretary of state and eventually president, serving two terms (1809–1817). He passed away on June 27, 1836, at the age of eighty-five, the last surviving signer of the Constitution. These two dedicated, diligent, and visionary men left, in the Bill of Rights they largely authored, a legacy of freedom that has and will continue profoundly to shape American life.

Strict Versus Loose Interpretations

Greenhaven's *The Bill of Rights: Opposing Viewpoints Digests* examines key facets of that legacy of freedom. The first chapter consists of a historical overview of the conflicting opinions in the original debate over the need for a bill of rights. The arguments of Madison, Mason, Hamilton, Henry, and other Federalists and Anti-Federalists are presented in the context of their time, specifically the months during which the states argued over ratifying the Constitution.

The subsequent chapters explore some of the legal and public debates about rights issues that have arisen over the years in the constantly expanding and evolving forum of American society. Although the founders reached an overall consensus of opinion about the meanings of the civil rights listed in the Constitution, later generations of legal and political scholars have continued to reinterpret those meanings. Some remain strict interpretationists, holding to rigid or "absolutist" readings of the Bill's articles. They say for example, that freedom of speech must be protected at all costs, no matter how ugly and provocative that speech might be. Opposing them are those who feel that the rights enumerated in the Constitution need to be reinterpreted in light of changing times and the advent of social situations and institutions the founders could not have foreseen. According to some looser, less rigid translations of the Bill of Rights, then, limitations must sometimes be put on free speech.

Rounding out this comprehensive overview of the history and key issues of the Bill of Rights is a useful appendix of original documents. Besides the Bill itself, included are excerpts from the English Bill of Rights and Virginia Declaration of Rights, both of which inspired the national version ratified in 1791. Also included are excerpts from key Supreme Court decisions involving important civil rights issues, for instance the questions of whether the death penalty constitutes cruel and unusual punishment and whether restricting free speech during wartime is justified. The ongoing debate over such issues represents part of the difficult but ultimately constructive struggle of a great democracy continuously reexamining itself and its constitutional heritage to meet the challenges of a rapidly changing world.

1. Eugene W. Hickok Jr., ed., "Introduction," *The Bill of Rights: Original Meaning and Current Understanding*. Charlottesville: University Press of Virginia, 1991, p. 1.

2. Fearing that a more centralized form of government might interfere with local rights and privileges, Rhode Island refused to send delegates; however, it did later ratify the Constitution on May 29, 1790, by a vote of 34 to 32.

3. Virginia Declaration of Rights, quoted in Edward Dumbauld, *The Bill of Rights and What It Means Today*. Westport, CT: Greenwood Press, 1979, pp. 171–72.

4. Excerpts from the Magna Carta, quoted in Eugen Weber, ed., *The Western Tradition: From the Ancient World to Louis XIV*. Boston: D.C. Heath, 1965, pp. 218–23.

5. Excerpts from the English Bill of Rights, quoted in Dumbauld, *The Bill of Rights and What It Means Today*, p. 168.

6. John Locke, *Second Treatise of Civil Government*, quoted in Saul K. Padover, ed., *Sources of Democracy: Voices of Freedom, Hope and Justice*. New York: McGraw-Hill, 1973, p. 211.

7. Milton C. Cummings Jr. and David Wise, *Democracy Under Pressure: An Introduction to the American Political Tradition*. New York: Harcourt Brace Jovanovich, 1974, p. 38.

8. Quoted in Catherine D. Bowen, *Miracle at Philadelphia: The Story of the Constitutional Convention, May to September 1787*. Boston: Little, Brown, 1966, p. 244.

9. The convention established that the Constitution would officially go into effect after nine of the thirteen states ratified it; however, it was widely understood that if the large states, particularly Virginia and New York, refused to ratify it, there could be no permanent Union or working government.

10. George Mason, "Objections to the Proposed Constitution," in J.R. Pole, ed., *The American Constitution, For and Against: The Federalist and Anti-Federalist Papers*. New York: Hill and Wang, 1987, pp. 126–28.

11. Alexander Hamilton, *The Federalist*, No. 84, quoted in Pole, *The American Constitution*, pp. 314–15.

12. Henry did so by using his influence with other Virginia legislators. This was possible because at the time senators were chosen by the state legislatures, rather than by popular votes (direct election of senators commenced with the passage of the Seventeenth Amendment in 1913).

13. Quoted in Robert Rutland, *James Madison: Founding Father*. New York: Macmillan, 1987, p. 47.

14. Quoted in Dumbauld, *The Bill of Rights and What It Means Today*, pp. 207–208.

15. Quoted in Dumbauld, *The Bill of Rights and What It Means Today*, p. 207.

16. Hickok, *The Bill of Rights*, p. 5.

17. In 1941 President Franklin D. Roosevelt recognized the historical importance of this date by proclaiming it Bill of Rights Day.

CHAPTER 1

Does the Constitution Need a Bill of Rights?

"In entering into the social compact, men ought not to leave their rulers at large, but erect a permanent landmark by which they may learn the extent of their authority, and the people be able to discover the first encroachments on their liberties."

The Constitution Needs a Bill of Rights

Author's Note: The arguments in this and the following essay are stated in the first person and presented in the context of their time, specifically the months following the 1787 Constitutional Convention. During this period, in which the state legislatures, press, and public at large argued loudly about whether or not to ratify the new Constitution, the most hotly debated issue among Federalists and Anti-Federalists was the possible inclusion of a bill of rights.

Without a doubt, the new Constitution requires a written bill of rights. Concerning the people's civil liberties, over which the split with Great Britain largely came about, the Constitution, comprising the blueprint for the new U.S. government, needs to be as comprehensive and clearly stated as possible. That way, long after the document's authors are dead, no American citizen will misunderstand their intent to safeguard the country's cherished freedoms for all times. As the popular pamphleteer who calls himself Brutus puts it to his fellow countrymen:

> The Constitution proposed . . . is designed not for
> yourselves alone, but for generations yet unborn.
> The principles, therefore, upon which the social
> compact is founded, ought to have been clearly and
> precisely stated, and the most express and full decla-
> ration of rights to have been made—But on this sub-
> ject there is almost an entire silence [in the
> Constitution].[1]

The most obvious and important reason a declaration of rights is needed is to restrain and counteract the potential abuses of power perpetrated by an overly strong federal government. As the honorable George Mason of Virginia has pointed out, the new government, as set forth in the Constitution, is a very potent one, its powers "being paramount to the laws and constitutions of the several states."[2] Simply put, the federal government might overrule the state governments on issues of individual rights. Brutus cites the example of the Constitution's Sixth Article, which states: "This Constitution and the Laws of the United States . . . shall be the supreme Law of the Land; and the Judges in every State shall be bound thereby, any Thing in the *Constitution*, or Laws of any State, *to the Contrary notwithstanding*" [italics added]. According to Brutus, this will have the effect of weakening the authority of the state constitutions. "It is," he says,

> not only necessarily implied . . . but positively
> expressed, that the different state constitutions are
> repealed and entirely done away, so far as they are
> inconsistent with this [article]. . . . Of what avail will
> the constitutions of the respective states be to pre-
> serve the rights of its citizens? should they be plead,
> the answer would be, the constitution of the United
> States . . . is the supreme law, and all legislatures and
> judicial officers . . . are bound by oath to support it.[3]

Thus, although several states have formulated their own bills of rights, these documents may not provide the needed security against an overbearing central government.

Some of those who remain unconvinced of the need for a bill of rights have asked the Anti-Federalists: What *are* these potential abuses that you worry the new federal government might inflict on states and individuals? Mr. Mason replies:

> The Congress may [if the current Constitution is enacted without a bill of rights] grant monopolies in trade and commerce, constitute new crimes, inflict unusual and severe punishments, and extend their power as far as they shall think proper; so that the state legislatures have no security for the powers now presumed to remain to them; or the people for their rights. There is no declaration of any kind for preserving the liberty of the press, the trial by jury in civil cases, nor against the danger of standing armies in time of peace.[4]

Pennsylvania legislator Robert Whitehill, who helped write that state's constitution in 1776, agrees, saying that if we could be absolutely sure that our governors would always do the right thing, then we would not need a bill of rights. However, as he so rightly points out, history has shown that even well-meaning rulers, once they are in possession of a great deal of power, often misuse it; and the most common result of that misuse is a curtailing of the people's personal liberties. "We know that it is the nature of power to seek its own augmentation [expansion]," Mr. Whitehill states,

> and thus the loss of liberty is the necessary consequence of a loose or extravagant delegation of authority. National freedom has been, and will be the sacrifice of ambition and power, and it is our duty to employ the present opportunity in stipulating such restrictions as are best calculated to protect us from oppression and slavery. . . . In entering into the social compact, men ought not to leave their rulers at large, but erect a permanent landmark by which they may learn the extent of their authority,

and the people be able to discover the first encroachments on their liberties.[5]

The "permanent landmark" of which Mr. Whitehill speaks is, of course, a bill of rights guaranteeing basic liberties. This is a much better way to discourage governmental abuse of the citizenry than that suggested by the Federalists—namely, when such an abuse occurs to convene a special convention of the states to deal with it. As the distinguished representative from Virginia, Mr. Patrick Henry, points out, those in power are likely not to allow such an assembly to gather in the first place:

> [The Federalists tell] us, that to prevent abuses in our government, we will assemble in convention, recall our delegated powers, and punish our servants for abusing the trust reposed in them. Oh sir, we should have fine times indeed, if to punish tyrants, it were only sufficient to assemble the people. [You will find this impossible when] your arms, wherewith you could defend yourselves, are gone. . . . Did you ever read about any revolution in any nation, brought about by the punishment of those in power, inflicted by those who had no power at all?[6]

Consider how much more effective it would be to have a bill of rights in place that could thwart potential tyrants before they have the chance to acquire dangerous or illegal powers. Thomas Jefferson, our ambassador to France, advocates, for instance, that such clearly enumerated rights would be a powerful weapon our Supreme Court justices could use to rein in individuals or groups that seem to threaten basic freedoms. He states:

> In the arguments in favor of a declaration of rights . . . one which has great weight with me [is] the legal check which it puts into the hands of the judiciary. This is a body, which, if rendered independent and kept strictly to their own department, merits great confidence for their learning and integrity.[7]

The erection of such legal barriers against the possible abuses of rulers is far from a new phenomenon. In his fervent appeal for the inclusion of a bill of rights in our federal Constitution, Brutus cites the obvious example of the country from which we have derived our origin:

Thomas Jefferson

> Their Magna Charta and Bill of Rights have long been the boast, as well as the security, of that nation. I need say no more, I presume, to an American, than, that this principle is a fundamental one, in all the constitutions of our own states. . . . From this it appears, that at a time when the pulse of liberty beat high and when an appeal was made to the people to form constitutions for the government of themselves, it was their universal sense, that such declarations should make a part of their frames of government. It is therefore the more astonishing, that this grand security to the rights of the people, is not to be found in this constitution.[8]

Mr. Jefferson is no less astonished and discomforted over the omission of a bill of rights. And his statement in a recent letter to Mr. James Madison is perhaps the most eloquent appeal yet formulated for including such a bill.

> I will now tell you what I do not like [about the new Constitution]. First, the omission of a bill of rights, providing clearly . . . for freedom of religion, freedom of the press, protection against standing armies, restriction of monopolies, the eternal and unremitting force of the habeas corpus laws, and

trials by jury in all matters of fact triable by the laws of the land, and not by the laws of nations. . . . I have a right to nothing which another has the right to take away; and [if we do not have a bill of rights] Congress will have a right to take away trials by jury in all civil cases. Let me add that a bill of rights is what the people are entitled to against every government on earth, general or particular; and what no just government should refuse, or rest on inference.[9]

So says Mr. Jefferson; and so, by God, should we all.

1. Brutus, "Essay of November 1, 1787," in J.R. Pole, ed., *The American Constitution, For and Against: The Federalist and Anti-Federalist Papers*. New York: Hill and Wang, 1987, p. 38. Most modern scholars believe that Brutus, whose Anti-Federalist essays appeared in the *New York Journal* between October 1787 and April 1788, was actually New York legislator Robert Yates, although positive evidence is still lacking.

2. George Mason, "Objections to the Proposed Constitution," in Pole, *The American Constitution*, p. 126.

3. Brutus, "Essay of November 1, 1787," quoted in Pole, *The American Constitution*, pp. 42–43.

4. Mason, "Objections," in Pole, *The American Constitution*, p. 128.

5. Robert Whitehill, "Speech of November 28, 1787, to Pennsylvania Legislature," quoted in William Dudley, ed., *The Bill of Rights: Opposing Viewpoints*. San Diego: Greenhaven Press, 1994, p. 30.

6. Patrick Henry, "Speech of June 5, 1788, to Virginia Ratifying Convention," quoted in Pole, *The American Constitution*, p. 120.

7. Thomas Jefferson, "Letter of March 15, 1789, to James Madison," quoted in Adrienne Koch and William Peden, eds., *The Life and Selected Writings of Thomas Jefferson*. New York: Random House, 1944, p. 462.

8. Brutus, "Essay of November 1, 1787," quoted in Pole, *The American Constitution*, pp. 39–40.

9. Thomas Jefferson, "Letter of December 20, 1787, to James Madison," quoted in Koch and Peden, *Thomas Jefferson*, pp. 437–38.

"A bill of rights annexed to a constitution, is an enumeration of the powers reserved. . . . Everything that is not enumerated, is presumed to be given. The consequence is, that an imperfect enumeration would throw all implied power into the scale of the government."

The Constitution Needs No Bill of Rights

Despite the fervent protestations of the Anti-Federalists, the new Constitution requires no special declaration of civil rights. It should be perfectly clear to all that the document, as written, already contains sufficient safeguards against potential governmental abuses of power. Mr. Edmund Randolph, one of Virginia's distinguished legislators, asks, "Why are the Bills of Rights distinct from the Constitution?" Answering his own question, he states that such bills should *not* be separate because such separateness implies some degree of inconsistency with the articles and intent of the Constitution itself. "If it be consistent with the Constitution, why not put it in the Constitution?" he inquires. And indeed, fulfilling the letter and spirit of that philosophy, all of the necessary concerns about civil rights have been addressed in the Constitution's existing articles. Here is how Mr. Randolph recently explained this fact to one of his leading opponents, Virginia's Patrick Henry:

The Honorable Gentleman has praised the Bill of Rights of Virginia, and called it his guardian angel, and vilified [condemned] this Constitution for not having it. . . . But let me ask the Gentleman where [in the Constitution] his favorite rights are violated? They are not violated by the tenth section, which contains restrictions on the States.[1] . . . Is there not provision made in this Constitution for the trial by jury in criminal cases? Does not the third article provide, that the trial of all crimes shall be by jury, and held in the State where the said crimes shall have been committed? Does it not follow, that the cause and nature of the accusation must be produced, because otherwise they cannot proceed on the case? Every one knows, that the witnesses must be brought before the jury, or else the prisoner will be discharged. . . . As to the exclusion of excessive bail and fines, and cruel and unusual punishments, this would follow of itself without a Bill of Rights.[2]

Mr. Randolph has also addressed the issue of freedom of the press, a right that many Anti-Federalists needlessly worry might be violated in the absence of a bill of rights. There plainly is no restriction on or limitation of the free press in the present Constitution, he asserts.

God forbid that I should give my voice against freedom of the press. But I ask . . . where is the page [in the Constitution] where it is restrained. If there had been any regulation about it, leaving it insecure, then there might have been reason for clamors. But this is not the case. If it be, I again ask for the particular clause which gives liberty to destroy the freedom of the press.[3]

Mr. Alexander Hamilton of New York heartily supports this view, saying that the state constitutions make little or no mention of freedom of the press. Yet in the years since these constitutions were drafted, no serious infringements of this freedom have occurred. This is because the spirit of the people and their legislators, all of whom recently broke with the mother country for abusing the rights of Americans, is too honorable to contemplate such despised actions. "What is the liberty of the press?" Hamilton inquires.

Alexander Hamilton

> Who can give it any definition which would not leave the utmost latitude for evasion? I hold it to be impracticable; and from this, I infer, that its security . . . must altogether depend on public opinion, and on the general spirit of the people and of the government. And here, after all . . . must we seek for the only solid basis of all our rights.[4]

Among the other civil rights issues that need not be addressed by a bill of rights is that of the creation of standing armies during peacetime. Americans have developed an exaggerated impression of this danger, probably in part, and perhaps justifiably, because of the recent war with Britain over the denial of certain liberties. Accordingly, those states that have enacted local bills of rights have included an article forbidding the raising of such armies WITHOUT THE CONSENT OF THE LEGISLATURE; and the Anti-Federalists have come to believe that without a similar declaration in a federal bill of rights, such armies will easily spring into existence. This, however, is an unwarranted fear. Mr. Hamilton holds that such declarations are unnecessary because

> the power of raising armies at all, under those [state] constitutions, can by no construction be deemed to reside any where else, than in the legislatures them-

selves; and it was superfluous, if not absurd, to declare that a matter should not be done without the consent of a body, which alone had the power of doing it.[5]

Mr. Hamilton has gone even further and stated that a federal bill of rights might be not only unnecessary, but even dangerous. Such a bill, he says, "would contain various exceptions to powers which are not granted; and on this account, would afford a . . . pretext to claim more than were granted."[6] Thus, a bill of rights designed to keep the government in its place might create a climate in which unscrupulous leaders could try to exercise powers not enumerated in the Constitution. The distinguished Pennsylvania legislator James Wilson here elaborates on this potential danger:

> In all societies, there are many powers and rights, which cannot be particularly enumerated. A bill of rights annexed to a constitution, is an enumeration of the powers reserved. . . . Everything that is not enumerated, is presumed to be given. The consequence is, that an imperfect enumeration would throw all implied power into the scale of the government; and the rights of the people would be rendered incomplete. On the other hand, an imperfect enumeration of the powers of the government, reserves all implied power to the people.[7]

Of these two choices, it is clearly much safer to risk giving the people more power by omitting a bill of rights, than to risk giving the government more power by including one.

"Parchment Barriers"

Even if this argument, erring on the side of caution, is exaggerated and a federal bill of rights would not be dangerous, such a bill would be, at the very least, ineffective. Virginia's James Madison, one of the Constitution's principal supporters, has pointed out that in the cases of the states' bills of rights, some of these "parchment barriers" have been repeatedly violated. And other violations could easily occur if a majority of citizens backed them. He is convinced, for example, that if most of his fellow Virginians belonged to a single religious sect, they would by now have established it as a state religion, regardless of the article in the state bill of rights prohibiting such an action. Mr. Madison adds that he sees no danger of the government becoming tyrannical. And even if this did come to pass, the provisions of a bill of rights would do little or nothing to remedy the situation. "Should a rebellion or insurrection alarm the people as well as the Government," he states, "and a suspension of the Habeas Corpus [right of an accused person to be formally charged in court] be dictated by the alarm, no written prohibitions on earth would prevent the measure."[8]

Still another reason not to add a bill of rights to the Constitution is that such a bill would make the latter too rigid. A rights declaration would purport to be unalterable; yet it is highly probable that later generations will want or need to change the Constitution. The honorable Noah Webster of Connecticut vehemently states:

> The [members of the] present generation have indeed a right to declare what *they* deem a *privilege*; but they have no right to say what the *next* generation shall deem a privilege. A State is a supreme corporation that never dies. . . . It has the same right to *repeal* a law this year, as it had to *make* it the last. If therefore our posterity are bound by our constitutions, and can neither amend nor annul them, they are to all intents and purposes our slaves. . . . The very attempt to make *perpetual* constitutions, is the assumption of a right to control the opinions of future generations; and to legislate for those over whom we have as little authority as we have over a nation in Asia.[9]

A federal bill of rights would thus be unnecessary, ineffective, potentially dangerous, and possibly unfair to our descendants; and we should leave the Constitution as it is.

1. Article I, Section 10, forbids any state from coining its own money, granting titles of nobility, imposing duties on imports and exports, keeping troops or warships in peacetime, signing agreements with foreign powers, and engaging in war ("unless actually invaded").

2. Edmund Randolph, "Speech of June 17, 1788, to Virginia Ratifying Convention," quoted in William Dudley, ed., *The Creation of the Constitution: Opposing Viewpoints*. San Diego: Greenhaven Press, 1995, pp. 243–44. Edmund Randolph had earlier refused to sign the Constitution because it lacked sufficient safeguards for civil liberties; however, in the months that followed, he changed his mind and supported the Constitution as written, out of a fear that if the document was not ratified, the Union might fall apart.

3. Randolph, "Speech of June 17, 1788," quoted in Dudley, *The Creation of the Constitution*, pp. 245–46.

4. Alexander Hamilton, *The Federalist, No. 84*, quoted in Harold C. Syrett, ed., *The Papers of Alexander Hamilton, Volume IV: January 1787–May 1788*. New York: Columbia University Press, 1962, p. 707.

5. Hamilton, *The Federalist, No. 26*, quoted in Syrett, *The Papers of Alexander Hamilton*, pp. 430–31.

6. Hamilton, *The Federalist, No. 84*, quoted in Syrett, *The Papers of Alexander Hamilton*, p. 706.

7. James Wilson, "Speech of November 28, 1787, to Pennsylvania Ratifying Convention," quoted in William Dudley, ed., *The Bill of Rights: Opposing Viewpoints*. San Diego: Greenhaven Press, 1994, p. 39.

8. James Madison, "Letter of October 24, 1787, to Thomas Jefferson," quoted in Dudley, *The Bill of Rights*, p. 46.

9. Noah Webster, "December 1787 Article for *American Magazine*," quoted in Dudley, *The Creation of the Constitution*, p. 247.

CHAPTER 2

Issues Concerning Freedom of Speech

"Were it left to me to decide whether we should have a government without newspapers, or newspapers without a government, I should not hesitate a moment to prefer the latter."

Freedom of Speech Should Be Protected at All Costs

The First Amendment's guarantees of freedom of speech and the press should be protected unconditionally and without exception. The amendment states quite clearly, "Congress shall make no law . . . abridging the freedom of speech, or of the press"; therefore, no laws should be passed abridging these rights. Renowned U.S. Supreme Court Justice Hugo L. Black, known for his "absolutist-literalist" interpretation of the First Amendment, puts it this way:

> I read "no law abridging" to mean *no law abridging.* The First Amendment, which is the supreme law of the land, has thus fixed its own value on freedom of speech and press by putting these freedoms wholly beyond the reach of *federal* power to abridge. No other provision of the Constitution purports to dilute the scope of these unequivocal commands of the First Amendment. Consequently, I do not believe that any federal agencies, including Congress and this Court, have power or authority to

subordinate speech and press to what they think are "more important interests."[1]

Justice Black's championing of freedom of expression is reminiscent of the views and actions of some of our most visionary founding fathers, who saw that a great democracy could not work without it. Writing to a colleague about the right to a completely free and uncensored press, Thomas Jefferson commented in 1787:

> The basis of our government being the opinion of the people, the very first object should be to keep that right; and were it left to me to decide whether we should have a government without newspapers, or newspapers without a government, I should not hesitate a moment to prefer the latter.[2]

Jefferson was right about the power of the people's opinion, which in the case of freedom of expression proved to be much like his own. Only a little more than a decade after he wrote the above words, that basic freedom faced its first crucial test in the form of the Sedition Act (1798), passed by the then ruling Federalist Party to silence the opposing Republican Party's appeal to the masses.[3] Under the Sedition Act, almost any public criticism of the president, Congress, or government in general was deemed a crime. Not surprisingly, the months that followed witnessed a resounding public outcry, as righteously indignant Americans of all walks of life condemned this unmitigated assault on the First Amendment. Responding to the will and mood of the people, after the hated act expired on March 3, 1801, President Jefferson (having recently taken office after the Republican victory in the 1800 election) pardoned all who had been convicted under it and dismissed the cases still awaiting trial.

So loudly had the people spoken against abridgment of free speech that more than a century passed before the government dared again to challenge the integrity of this liberty. A number of twentieth-century federal and state laws have attempted to curb free speech in one way or another, and most of these have resulted in appeals to the Supreme Court. None, including those the Court has upheld, are constitutional under a strict, absolutist reading of the First Amendment.

The first major modern case, *Schenck v. United States* (1919), well illustrates this point. During World War I, Charles Schenck, secretary of the Socialist Party, was found guilty of conspiring to obstruct armed forces recruiting through the distribution of a pamphlet attacking conscription.[4] When he appealed to the high court, the justices voted unanimously to uphold his conviction. Writing for the Court, Justice Oliver W. Holmes explained that the "dangerous circumstances" surrounding the country's involvement in the war had dictated the decision: "The character of every act depends upon the circumstances in which it is done. . . . The most stringent protection of free speech would not protect a man in falsely shouting fire in a theater and causing a panic."[5] This opinion established the "clear and present danger" doctrine that received increasing acceptance in the decades that followed.

Unanimous or not, the decision was unfair; the Court's opinion—that Mr. Schenck's pamphlet constituted an imminent threat to the country—was extreme and highly exaggerated. To suggest that a single circular distributed to a few thousand people in a small section of the country could endanger the fighting ability of the entire national military establishment is ludicrous. Writing less than a decade later, Justice Louis D. Brandeis stated that:

> Only an emergency can justify repression. . . .
> Moreover, even immediate danger cannot justify
> resort to prohibition of . . . functions essential to
> effective democracy, unless the evil apprehended is
> relatively serious. Prohibition of free speech . . . is a
> measure so stringent that it would be inappropriate
> as a means of averting a relatively trivial harm to
> society.[6]

The widely respected Justice Wiley B. Rutledge later agreed with and extended this view, saying, "Only the gravest abuses, endangering paramount interests, give occasion for permissible limitation [of free speech]."[7]

The fact is that at no time in U.S. history have the "paramount interests" of the country been remotely threatened enough to justify curbing the First Amendment. And even if a truly grave threat did occur (say, for instance, an ongoing invasion of U.S. soil by a foreign foe), restricting freedom of speech would still be an extreme and reprehensible act. The eminent philosopher and First Amendment scholar Alexander Meiklejohn persuasively stated this view in 1945:

> No one who reads with care the text of the First Amendment can fail to be startled by its absoluteness. The phrase, "Congress shall make no law . . . abridging freedom of speech," is unqualified. It admits no exceptions. To say that no laws . . . shall be made means that no laws . . . shall, under any circumstances, be made. That prohibition holds good in war as in peace, in danger as in security.[8]

This absolute prohibition, after all, is what founders like Jefferson intended when they amended the Constitution, and what the American people affirmed in their fervent denunciation of the 1798 Sedition Act. About the founders, Brandeis wrote:

> They valued liberty both as an end and as a means. . . . They believed that freedom to think as you will and to speak as you think are means indispensable to the discovery and spread of political truth; that without free speech . . . discussion would be futile . . . that fear breeds repression; that repression breeds hate; that hate menaces stable government; that the path to safety lies in the opportunity to discuss freely supposed grievances and proposed remedies.[9]

And as for the people, thanks to the First Amendment they have the right to speak out, no matter how seemingly dangerous, outrageous, or offensive the expression; for this liberty, perhaps more than any other, defines what it means to be truly free.

1. Hugo L. Black, *Smith v. California* (1959), quoted in Lucius J. Barker and Twiley W. Barker Jr., eds., *Civil Liberties and the Constitution: Cases and Commentaries*. Englewood Cliffs, NJ: Prentice-Hall, 1975, p. 89.

2. Thomas Jefferson, "Letter of January 16, 1787, to Colonel Edward Carrington," quoted in Adrienne Koch and William Peden, eds., *The Life and Selected Writings of Thomas Jefferson*. New York: Random House, 1944, pp. 411–12.

3. The Republican Party of that era was not the same as today's party of the same name. The early Republican Party slowly evolved into the modern Democratic Party; while the modern Republican Party formed in the 1850s, principally at first to oppose the spread of slavery into the western territories.

4. The law broken was a new Sedition Act, passed in 1918 as an extension of the 1917 Espionage Act.

5. Oliver W. Holmes, *Schenck v. United States* (1919), quoted in Andrew D. Weinberger, *Freedom and Protection: The Bill of Rights*. San Francisco: Chandler Publishing, 1962, p. 91.

6. Louis D. Brandeis, *Whitney v. California* (1927), quoted in Edward Dumbauld, *The Bill of Rights and What It Means Today*. Westport, CT: Greenwood Press, 1979, pp. 116–17.

7. Wiley B. Rutledge, *Thomas v. Collins* (1945), quoted in Barker and Barker, *Civil Liberties and the Constitution*, p. 86.

8. Alexander Meiklejohn, *Free Speech and Its Relation to Self-Government*. New York: Harper and Brothers, 1948, p. 17.

9. Brandeis, *Whitney v. California*, quoted in William Dudley, ed., *The Bill of Rights: Opposing Viewpoints*. San Diego: Greenhaven Press, 1994, p. 100.

"Every society has a right to preserve public peace and order, and therefore has a good right to prohibit the propagation of opinions which have a dangerous tendency."

Limitations Must Sometimes Be Placed on Freedom of Speech

There is no doubt that freedom of speech is an important and cherished liberty, constituting one of the cornerstones of a great democracy like the United States. And this freedom should certainly not be curbed lightly or frivolously. However, the fact is that certain special, extreme, or dangerous situations occasionally exist in which society must place limits on the First Amendment in order to preserve itself and the safety of its citizens. Law-abiding citizens who simply disagree with the government and seek peaceful change should enjoy the complete and unrestricted protection of the free speech statute. But extremists who advocate change through violent overthrow of the government or destruction of public institutions should not be allowed the same protection; in short, we must not allow such persons to take advantage of the system so that they can then proceed to destroy it. The distinguished legal scholar John H. Wigmore wrote in 1920:

> The truth is that the constitutional guarantee of freedom of speech is being invoked more and more in misuse. It represents the unfair protection much

44

desired by impatient and fanatical minorities—
fanatically committed to some new revolutionary
belief, and impatient of the usual process of ratio-
nally converting the majority. . . . These fanatical
leaders invoke club-law. They call for "direct action"
(this cowardly euphemism for brutal mob-violence
must now be familiar to all readers of recent period-
ical literature). And when their urgent propaganda
of club-law meets lawful interference, they invoke
the sacred constitutional guarantee of "freedom of
speech." It is simply a profanation of that term.[1]

Professor Wigmore's rational view of a free society retain-
ing the right and ability to protect itself from violent attack is
not new. The great eighteenth-century English essayist
Samuel Johnson supported basic freedoms but also recognized practical limitations in their application. While people
often need protection from government, he suggests, government sometimes needs protection from people. Johnson
writes: "Every society has a right to preserve public peace and
order, and therefore has a good right to prohibit the propagation of opinions which have a dangerous tendency."[2] In the
same spirit, in 1805 Thomas Jefferson, one of history's
staunchest advocates of personal liberties, including freedom
of the press, recognized that a "licentious" and "abusive" press
might hurt society. While suggesting that the most practical
and time-effective way to curb such abuse was the "censorship
of public opinion," he added:

> No inference is here intended, that the laws provid-
> ed by the State against false and defamatory publi-
> cations, should not be enforced; he who has time,
> renders a service to public morals and public tran-
> quillity, in reforming these abuses by the salutary
> coercions [beneficial enforcement] of the law.[3]

The twentieth century has seen its share of societal dangers
that needed to be quelled by such "beneficial enforcement" of

laws designed to maintain public order and the common good. The Supreme Court's unanimous upholding of the conviction of Charles Schenck in 1919 affords a clear example. Schenck distributed more than fifteen thousand circulars attacking the conscription of American soldiers in World War I, a crime that, had it been allowed to continue, might have seriously hampered the war effort and endangered American lives. Speaking for his colleagues, Justice Oliver W. Holmes stated:

> We admit that in many places and in ordinary times the defendants in saying all that was said in the circular would have been within their constitutional rights. But the character of every act depends upon the circumstances in which it is done. . . . The most stringent protection of free speech would not protect a man in falsely shouting fire in a theater and causing a panic. . . . The question in every case is whether the words used are in such circumstances and are of such nature as to create a clear and present danger that they will bring about the substantive evils that Congress has a right to prevent. It is a question of proximity and degree. When a nation is at war many things that might be said in time of peace are such a hindrance to its effort that their utterance will not be endured so long as men fight, and that no Court could regard them as protected by any constitutional right.[4]

The high court applied this reasonable doctrine of "clear and present danger," with varying effectiveness, in later similar cases, especially involving communist conspiracies to topple the U.S. government. One of the most infamous of these cases was *Dennis v. United States* (1951). Eleven Communist Party leaders were convicted of advocating the overthrow of the government; and in a six-to-two vote (one justice not participating and two justices dissenting), the Court upheld the conviction.[5] One of the dissenters, Justice William O. Douglas, later claimed that this decision was unfair because in the United States "in the early 1950s there was no remote possibility" of a small group of communists overthrowing the government; that these were mere "peddlers of unwanted ideas . . . the most unpopular people in the land, incapable of commanding enough votes to get elected to any office, no matter how lowly."[6]

However, Chief Justice Frederick M. Vinson persuasively countered this view, saying that the argument that the government "is strong [and] possesses ample powers to put down" so tiny a group of revolutionaries "with ease" is "not the question." Even if a rebellion is doomed to failure from the outset, he wrote in the case's majority opinion, the precedent such an insurrection might set is sufficiently evil for Congress to enact preventative laws. Vinson further stated:

> In this case we are squarely presented with the application of the "clear and present danger" test, and must decide what that phrase imports. . . . Overthrow of the government by force and violence is certainly a substantial enough interest for the government to limit speech. Indeed, this is the ultimate value of any society, for if a society cannot protect its very structure from armed internal attack, it must follow that no subordinate value can be protected. . . . Obviously, the words ["clear and present danger"] cannot mean that before the government may act, it must wait until the *putsch* [coup, or overthrow] is about to be executed, the plans have been made and signal is awaited. If government is aware that a group aiming at its overthrow is attempting to indoctrinate its members and to commit them to a course . . . [of violence], action by the government is required.[7]

Regarding this logical and reasonable point—that the government should not wait until serious harm is already done before acting—Vinson and his assenting colleagues were on firm ground. Justice Edward T. Sanford had written in an earlier case:

The effect of a given utterance cannot be accurately foreseen. The state cannot reasonably be required to measure the danger from every such utterance in the nice balance of a jeweler's scale. A single revolutionary spark may kindle a fire that, smoldering for a time, may burst into a sweeping and destructive conflagration. It cannot be said that the state is acting arbitrarily or unreasonably when ... it seeks to extinguish the spark without waiting until it has enkindled the flame or blazed into the conflagration.[8]

Thus, while all law-abiding citizens are entitled to free speech, that constitutional liberty does not give them the right to immunity from every possible use of language, no matter how dangerous. One person's freedom of speech should not be so absolute that it allows him or her to threaten and destroy a government that grants wide-ranging freedoms to all, and thereby to rob everyone else of those liberties.

1. John H. Wigmore, *"Abrams v. United States*: Freedom of Speech and Freedom of Thuggery in War-Time and Peace-Time," quoted in William Dudley, ed., *The Bill of Rights: Opposing Viewpoints*. San Diego: Greenhaven Press, 1994, p. 93.

2. Quoted in William O. Douglas, *The Right of the People*. Garden City, NY: Doubleday, 1958, p. 45.

3. Thomas Jefferson, *Second Inaugural Address* (March 4, 1805), quoted in Adrienne Koch and William Peden, eds., *The Life and Selected Writings of Thomas Jefferson*. New York: Random House, 1944, p. 343.

4. Oliver W. Holmes, *Schenck v. United States* (1919), quoted in Andrew D. Weinberger, *Freedom and Protection: The Bill of Rights*. San Francisco: Chandler Publishing, 1962, pp. 91–92.

5. The men were convicted under the conspiracy provisions of the 1940 Smith Act.

6. Douglas, *The Right of the People*, p. 51.

7. Frederick M. Vinson, *Dennis v. United States* (1951), quoted in Milton R. Konvitz, ed., *Bill of Rights Reader: Leading Constitutional Cases*. Ithaca, NY: Cornell University Press, 1960, p. 255.

8. Edward T. Sanford, *Gitlow v. New York* (1925), quoted in Lucius J. Barker and Twiley W. Barker Jr., eds., *Civil Liberties and the Constitution: Cases and Commentaries*. Englewood Cliffs, NJ: Prentice-Hall, 1975, p. 87.

"Implicit in the history of the First Amendment is the rejection of obscenity as utterly without redeeming social importance. . . . We hold that obscenity is not within the area of constitutionally protected speech or press."

Censorship Is Sometimes Necessary for the Public Good

The very idea of censorship often inspires strong emotional outcries and arguments from many people who fear that putting some restrictions on a particular book, magazine, movie, or Internet access site will rob them of their right to free speech and press under the wording of the First Amendment. Yet no one who advocates some form of censorship desires to erode or cripple that or any other section of the Bill of Rights. What they do want is to make society a little cleaner and safer for the vast majority of law-abiding and respectable people who have no interest in explicitly obscene or violent material. The sad fact is that a tiny minority of individuals, driven by the profit motive, twisted social values, or both, consistently flood the media with such material. It is both fitting and necessary for society to protect itself, and especially the minds of its children, from potentially harmful kinds of expression. As Washington, D.C., librarian Thomas Storck phrases it, "Censorship has long seemed to me a necessary, if regrettable, part of practical political wisdom and an opportunity for the judicious exercise of human intelligence."[1]

That obscene and violent material is potentially harmful, particularly to children, who are very impressionable, is a matter both of common sense and documented experience. "Human nature being what it is," Storck writes, "it is naive to think we can freely read and view things that promote or portray evil deeds without sometimes feeling encouraged to commit such deeds."[2] Indeed, the realization that bad words and bad images can inspire bad actions lies at the very core of the occasional need for judiciously applied censorship of various forms of media. Monsignor Joseph Howard, former executive officer for the National Office for Decent Literature, asks:

> Is it unreasonable to argue . . . that if a devotional work can inspire, the works of [the Marquis] de Sade [an eighteenth-century French writer known for his explicit depictions of sex] can degrade? If a [public] medium [such as a magazine] can sell Cadillacs to a man, can it not peddle contraceptives to his son? If a biography can make a youngster want to be a Mickey Mantle . . . can it not also make him aspire to be a . . . Jack the Ripper? If a masterpiece of art can bring a lump to the throat, couldn't a different picture produce a different reaction?[3]

Unfortunately, all of these questions must be answered in the affirmative. The old adage of "monkey see, monkey do" is all too often translated into stark reality in the form of "copycat" crimes enacted in communities across the land. These and other signs of society's moral decay frequently derive from imitative behavior, which is natural to everyone but especially to children, who model most of their actions on those of the adults they encounter in person or in the media. According to Sidney Callahan, a columnist for *Commonweal* magazine:

> Violent images on TV or in the movies have inspired people to set spouses on fire in their beds,

lie down in the middle of highways, extort money by placing bombs in airplanes, rape people in particularly disgusting ways, and who knows how many other kinds of shootings and assaults. . . . Most psychologists who have studied the question of how aggression operates are convinced that everyone learns violent behavior by seeing it enacted, ready or not. Children will beat . . . dolls into the ground if they have seen grown-ups do it first, and even those children who do not immediately enact the aggression learn the behavior and remember how it's done. The more prestigious the person modeling aggressive behavior, the more likely it is to be imitated by observers. Imitation, after all, is an indispensable way that an intelligent species like ours learns.[4]

Thus, in varying degrees we become what we absorb through our everyday experience, just as, in a very real sense, we become what we eat; and as good and wholesome images can lead to good deeds, sick and unwholesome images can lead to bad deeds. Perhaps the most obvious and insidious example of this process is the link between obscene or pornographic material and sexual violence. "Pornography is intended to arouse sexual appetite—one of the most volatile appetites of human nature," states Charles Keating, who served on President Nixon's Federal Commission on Obscenity and Pornography. "Once that appetite is aroused, it will seek satisfaction; and the satisfaction sought, without proper moral restraints, is often reflected in the social statistics [of venereal disease, illegitimacy, promiscuity, and divorce]."[5] Anyone who doubts the existence of this link between pornography and crime need only remember the words of one of this century's greatest law-enforcement experts, former FBI director J. Edgar Hoover:

Police officials . . . unequivocally state that lewd and obscene material plays a motivating role in sexual violence. In case after case, the sex criminal has on

his person or in his possession pornographic literature or pictures. . . . Such filth in the hands of young
people and curious adolescents does untold damage
and leads to disastrous consequences.[6]

It was this sort of damage, no doubt, that the Supreme
Court had in mind when, in 1957, it upheld the conviction of
a New York smut shop owner whose mailing of obscene circulars had violated a federal obscenity statute (*Roth v. United
States*). The Court majority held that the proper test for
obscenity was whether or not the material would arouse
impure sexual thoughts in the average person in the community. Most importantly, writing for the majority, Justice
William J. Brennan stated that obscenity is not protected by
the First Amendment:

All ideas having even the slightest redeeming social
importance—unorthodox ideas, controversial ideas,
even ideas hateful to the prevailing climate of opinion—have the full protection of the [First
Amendment's] guaranties. . . . But implicit in the history of the First Amendment is the rejection of

Mike Ramirez. Reprinted by permission of Copley News Service.

obscenity as utterly without redeeming social importance. This rejection for that reason is mirrored in the universal national agreement of over 50 nations, in the obscenity laws of all the . . . states, and in the 20 obscenity laws enacted by the Congress from 1842 to 1956. . . . We hold that obscenity is not within the area of constitutionally protected speech or press.[7]

Regardless of community laws or Supreme Court rulings, of course, pornographers have found ways to stay in business, to continue to corrupt the morals of those in the community who are most susceptible, particularly children. In the decades since the *Roth* ruling, regrettably, the high court has softened its stance against obscenity; and many local authorities have accepted the false assumption that mere regulation will do the trick. Typically, smut shops are confined to narrow "combat" districts in cities, and X-rated videos are kept in "adults only" rooms in the backs of video stores. Supposedly, such measures will keep such filth out of the hands of impressionable minors. Yet everyone knows that children easily circumvent these ineffective barriers every day; and because this exposure causes some of these children to become sexual criminals, society continues to pay the price.[8]

A New Threat to Decency

Moreover, rapidly evolving technology is regularly creating new markets, representing fresh opportunities for smut mongers to hook new generations of unsuspecting young people. The computer "information superhighway," or Internet, is a prominent example. A child can get on the Internet, says concerned Nebraska senator Jim Exon, "and freely ride to on-line 'red light districts' that contain some of the most perverse and depraved pornographic material available." How can we protect our children, and ultimately society in general, from this new threat to decency? Senator Exon answers:

Access for children can be restricted in several ways, including requiring use of a verified credit card, debit account, adult access code or adult personal identification number. The Supreme Court already has approved such means for limiting child access to telephone "dial-a-porn" services.[9]

Although these measures will surely help, we need to go further. As Senator Exon and other responsible leaders advocate, we need to add the deterrent of law, constituting a minimal level of censorship that does not infringe on the free speech of the vast majority. This is the sane and responsible way to create a more effective barrier against those who think nothing of destroying society's soul for a buck.

1. Thomas Storck, "A Case for Censorship," quoted in Byron L. Stay, ed., *Censorship: Opposing Viewpoints*. San Diego: Greenhaven Press, 1997, p. 18.

2. Storck, "A Case for Censorship," quoted in Stay, *Censorship*, p. 18.

3. Monsignor Joseph Howard, quoted in Harold H. Hart, ed., *Censorship: For and Against*. New York: Hart Publishing, 1971, p. 31. The National Office for Decent Literature, or NODL, a watchdog organization formed out of concern over threats to societal morals, operated from 1938 to 1969 under the sponsorship of the Catholic Bishops of America.

4. Sidney Callahan, "What We See, We Do," quoted in Stay, *Censorship*, p. 154.

5. Charles Keating, quoted in Hart, *Censorship*, pp. 109–10.

6. J. Edgar Hoover, quoted in Hart, *Censorship*, p. 29.

7. William J. Brennan, *Roth v. United States* (1957), quoted in Milton R. Konvitz, ed., *Bill of Rights Reader: Leading Constitutional Cases*. Ithaca, NY: Cornell University Press, 1960, p. 548.

8. For more detailed information about the harmful effects of obscene materials on children and how such materials might be regulated or banned, contact the National Coalition for the Protection of Children and Families, 800 Compton Rd., Suite 9224, Cincinnati, OH 45231, (513) 521–6227, and/or Parents Alliance to Protect Our Children, 44 E. Tacoma Ave., Latrobe, PA 15650, (412) 459–9076; both organizations publish helpful pamphlets and position papers that are available on request.

9. Senator Jim Exon, "Only the Force of Law Can Deter Pornographers," quoted in Stay, *Censorship*, pp. 126–28.

"Under our system of government there is an accommoda-
tion for the widest variety of tastes and ideas. . . . The
requirement that literature or art conform to some norm
prescribed by an official smacks of an ideology foreign to
our system."

Censorship of Any Kind Violates the First Amendment

Those who advocate censorship of books, films, and other forms of media claim that "obscenity," "pornography," and "filth" poison public morals and lead to violence, sex crimes, and other antisocial behavior. Thus, they say, we need stricter laws banning such "lewd" materials. According to this view, such laws do not infringe on the free speech and press protections of the First Amendment because that statute does not protect obscenity, which "has no redeeming social value."

This view is unfounded for a number of reasons. First, it is extremely difficult to define obscenity. Often, what one individual deems lewd and filthy, others see as interesting, entertaining, or perhaps just boring; and views of what is and is not obscene vary markedly from one society to another, and within a single society from one century or even one decade to another.

The rapidly changing views of the U.S. Supreme Court on the subject constitute a clear example. In *Roth v. United States*, a 1957 case in which the Court upheld the conviction of a store owner who sent explicitly sexual materials through the mail, the majority held that material is obscene if "to the average person, applying contemporary community standards, the dominant theme of the material taken as a whole appeals to prurient [lewd] interest."[1] Later, the Court modified this view, saying that to be obscene, material must be "patently offensive" as well as prurient (*Manual Enterprises v. Day*, 1962);[2] later still it decided that what may be obscene for minors may not be so for adults (*Ginsberg v. New York*, 1968);[3] and in 1969 the Court unanimously declared that personal use of obscene material by an adult in his or her home is not a crime (*Stanley v. Georgia*). Not only have legal views about obscenity changed, but the wording of such views remains general, vague, and applicable only to selected segments of the population. What constitutes the "average person" mentioned in the *Roth* ruling? Cannot "lewdness" have widely different meanings to different people?

Censorship Is Unneeded and Ineffective

Another reason that censorship is unfounded is that it is both unneeded and ineffective. Sexually explicit books, magazines, films, and so forth have been widely available to those seeking them for most of this century, despite many laws aimed at suppressing them; and, at the very least, tens of millions of people, including many minors, have viewed them. Why, then, are there not millions of violent sex offenders laying waste to society? In fact, such criminals consistently remain a tiny minority of the population.

Indeed, no substantive evidence has been found establishing that a direct causal link exists between sexually explicit materials and crime. Finding such materials in the homes of sex offenders, a situation often loudly cited by censorship advocates, is irrelevant. These sick individuals, deeply confused, troubled, and angry about sexual and other issues, may at times channel their pent-up urges and aggressions into various outlets, among them viewing sexually explicit materials and committing criminal acts; and in such situations the materials, like the acts, must be seen as an effect, rather than a cause, of their psychological problems.[4]

Censorship is also unfounded because it violates the First Amendment and is therefore unconstitutional. Although a Supreme Court majority supported a form of censorship in the famous *Roth v. United States* case, the minority view in that case has, over time, proven to be more in tune with the feelings and needs of most Americans. Writing for the minority, Justice William O. Douglas stated:

> The test of obscenity the Court endorses today gives the censor free range over a vast domain. To allow the state to step in and punish mere speech or publication that the judge or the jury thinks has an *undesirable* impact on thoughts but that is not shown to be part of unlawful action is drastically to curtail the First Amendment. . . . The standard of what offends

Reprinted by permission of Steve Kelley.

> "the common conscience of the community" con-
> flicts, in my judgment, with the command of the
> First Amendment that "Congress shall make no law
> . . . abridging the freedom of speech, or of the
> press." Certainly that standard would not be an
> acceptable one if religion, economics, politics or
> philosophy were involved. How does it become a
> constitutional standard when literature treating with
> sex is concerned?[5]

Ironically, Douglas had already successfully defended First
Amendment protection of literature in an earlier case, saying,
"Under our system of government there is an accommodation
for the widest variety of tastes and ideas. . . . The requirement
that literature or art conform to some norm prescribed by an
official smacks of an ideology foreign to our system."[6] In the
same spirit, in 1959 the Court rejected the attempted ban of
the film *Lady Chatterley's Lover*. The idea, said Justice Potter
Stewart, that such a ban was justified because the movie "por-
trays a relationship [adultery] which is contrary to the moral
standards" of society, "misconceives what it is that the
Constitution protects." The First Amendment's guaranties, he
explained, are "not confined to the expression of ideas that are
conventional or shared by the majority."[7]

Still another reason that censorship is unfair, unjust, and
un-American is that it presupposes that the censor is somehow
qualified to set standards of taste and decency for everyone
else. If viewing a certain book or film is supposedly harmful or
corrupting, how or why is the censor immune to such corrup-
tion? Does he or she purport to possess intellect, taste, and a
sense of right and wrong that are superior to those of the rest
of us? William O. Douglas answers:

> Once the censor enters the scene, he becomes by
> virtue of his power the dictator. . . . The practical
> exigencies [demands] of a system of censorship
> means that the author writes to the standards of the
> censor, who is beyond effective control. He writes

to avoid the censor's prejudices and displeasure, if not to please him. The censor becomes the great leveler of thought. The censor sets a deadening pattern of conformity which one must meet or go out of business.[8]

The following exchange from the testimony of a 1961 case, in which the city of Chicago defended its right to approve and license films before their public exhibition, is disturbingly revealing about the mind and methods of the typical censor:

Q: Am I to understand that the procedure is that only these six people [the city's official censors] are in the room, and perhaps you [the chief censor], at the time the film is shown?

A: Yes.

Q: Does the [film's] distributor ever get a chance to present his views on the picture?

A: No, sir.

Q: Are other people's views invited, such as drama critics or movie reviewers or writers or artists of some kind; or are they ever asked to comment on the film before the censor board makes its decision?

A: No, sir.

Q: In other words, it is these six people plus yourself . . . who decide whether the picture conforms to the standards set up in the [city] ordinance?

A: Yes, sir.[9]

In this and all other instances of censorship, what society can see and experience is dictated by the personal opinions, feelings, tastes, worries, and fears of one or a handful of individuals. There is something inherently odd and disquieting about a person who wants or feels compelled to become a censor; for such people usually do so to promote some personal agenda. "If we took censors at face value," writes Carey McWilliams, former editor of the *Nation*,

we would believe that they are genuinely concerned about the harmful effect certain materials
may have on others . . . and on society at large. But
censors do not understand their own motivations.
For the most part, they are motivated by fear. To a
degree, fear that certain materials may have harmful effects on others . . . is genuine; but the real fear
stems from a fear that the censor has about himself,
about his own impulses and desires. If looking at
nude photographs bothers him, he feels that it
must have the same effect on others. . . . He feels
that others must be protected, as he would protect
himself.[10]

Protecting children from materials that they may not yet be
old enough to understand and properly evaluate is a perfectly
appropriate task that should be undertaken by parents. But
grown-ups do not need censors taking on the role of parents
for society. Adults have the right, guaranteed by the First
Amendment, to view whatever they please and to decide for
themselves whether the material is worthwhile or not.

Reprinted by permission of Craig MacIntosh.

1. William J. Brennan, *Roth v. United States* (1957), quoted in Milton R. Konvitz, ed., *Bill of Rights Reader: Leading Constitutional Cases*. Ithaca, NY: Cornell University Press, 1960, p. 549.

2. This ruling overturned an obscenity conviction of a man who sent magazines containing photos of nude males through the mail.

3. "The state has an independent interest in the well-being of its youth," wrote Justice Brennan, and can therefore give them "a more restricted right than that assured to adults." (Quoted in Lucius J. Barker and Twiley W. Barker Jr., eds., *Civil Liberties and the Constitution: Cases and Commentaries*. Englewood Cliffs, NJ: Prentice-Hall, 1975, p. 120.)

4. For more detailed information about the use, misuse, and efforts to censor sexually explicit materials, see Marjorie Heins, *Sex, Sin, and Blasphemy: A Guide to America's Censorship Wars*. New York: New Press, 1993; and/or contact the Fund for Free Expression, 485 Fifth Ave., New York, NY 10017, (212) 972–8400, and the National Coalition Against Censorship (NCAC), 275 Seventh Ave., 20th Floor, New York, NY 10001, (212) 807–6222.

5. William O. Douglas, *Roth v. United States* (1957), quoted in Konvitz, *Bill of Rights Reader*, pp. 558–59.

6. William O. Douglas, writing the Court's unanimous opinion in the 1946 *Hannegan v. Esquire* case, quoted in Konvitz, *Bill of Rights Reader*, p. 516; the Court found in favor of *Esquire* magazine, which the U.S. Postmaster General had attempted to ban from the mails for being "vulgar" and "in poor taste."

7. Potter Stewart, *Kingsley International Pictures Corp. v. Regents of University of State of New York* (1959), quoted in Konvitz, *Bill of Rights Reader*, p. 584.

8. William O. Douglas, *The Right of the People*. Garden City, NY: Doubleday, 1958, pp. 66–67.

9. From the dissenting opinion of Chief Justice Earl Warren in *Times Film v. Chicago* (1961), quoted in Andrew D. Weinberger, *Freedom and Protection: The Bill of Rights*. San Francisco: Chandler Publishing, 1962, p. 133.

10. Carey McWilliams, quoted in Harold H. Hart, ed., *Censorship: For and Against*. New York: Hart Publishing, 1971, pp. 84–85.

CHAPTER 3

Differing Interpretations of Due Process of Law

"I would follow what I believe was the original purpose of the Fourteenth Amendment—to extend to all the people of the nation the complete protection of the Bill of Rights."

Due Process Should Include All Sections of the Bill of Rights

Arguments over the meaning of the phrase "due process of law" in the Fifth Amendment of the Bill of Rights have raged ever since that historic document was ratified in 1791. The amendment's various clauses stipulate that a person must be accorded the right to face a grand jury before being convicted of a capital crime such as murder; that no one can be tried twice for the same crime (double jeopardy); that no person can be forced to testify against him- or herself; nor can anyone "be deprived of life, liberty, or property, without due process of law." Some judges, legislators, and scholars have interpreted the due process clause very narrowly. They say that the founders meant the clause to stand by itself and that it does not refer to or include the rights mentioned in the other clauses. Nor, they say, does it include any of the rights mentioned in the Bill's other amendments.

However, this interpretation is too restrictive. Regardless of their exact (or inexact?) wording, in creating the Bill of Rights, the founders set out to enumerate a wide range of personal liberties. These rights should not be viewed as having nothing to do with one another. According to law, when a person is arrested for a crime, he or she goes through a step-by-step process—indictment, trial by jury, conviction (or acquittal), sentencing, appeals, and so on. That person's legal rights, as listed in the Fifth and some other amendments, are an intrinsic part of this overall criminal justice procedure.

For example, the rights to a speedy trial and to be confronted with the witnesses against oneself are listed in the Sixth Amendment; yet these are intimately related to the provisions of the Fifth Amendment, and the provisions of both amendments comprise various facets of the same legal process. "The rights, for the security of which these express provisions were made," commented Supreme Court Justice John M. Harlan in 1884,

> were of a character so essential to the safety of the people that it was deemed wise to avoid the possibility that Congress, in regulating the processes of law, would impair or destroy them. Hence, their specific enumeration in the earlier amendments of the Constitution, in connection with the general requirement of due process of law, the latter itself being broad enough to cover every right of life, liberty or property secured by the settled usages and modes of [legal] proceeding existing under the common and statute law of England at the time our government was founded.[1]

It seems incredible today that when Justice Harlan expressed this very reasonable, fair, and logical opinion, he was the lone dissenting voice in a high court ruling that rejected a broad, inclusive interpretation of due process. That landmark case, *Hurtado v. California*, pitted the provisions of the Fifth Amendment against those of the Fourteenth Amendment, passed in 1868.[2] The Fourteenth Amendment declares that the states must uphold the civil rights of their respective citizens, stating in part that "No State [shall] . . . deprive any person of life, liberty, or property, without due process of law." The Court had to decide what due process really meant. Did the mention of due process in the Fourteenth Amendment mean that the states were subject to the same provisions laid out in the Bill of Rights, which had previously applied to federal cases only? "The lines of judicial battle were thus clearly drawn," writes legal scholar Joel M. Gora.

> On one side was the view of the *Hurtado* majority that the due process guarantee in the Fourteenth Amendment was to be interpreted flexibly, with English law traditions serving only as a guide, and with the specific guarantees of the original Bill of Rights not automatically embodied as part of the due process clause. On the other side was Justice Harlan's view that these specific guarantees were essential to the meaning of "due process of law," that they limited the states to no less than the federal government, and that the preservation of liberty was better assured by adherence to those specifics than by a flexible judicial interpretation.[3]

The narrow view of due process taken by the *Hurtado* majority amounted to a gaping loophole allowing individual states to deny people some of the liberties guaranteed in the Bill of Rights; and this loophole prevailed for more than a half century. Fortunately, however, it eventually began to erode, thanks in part to the *Adamson v. California* decision in 1947. A Los Angeles man refused to testify at his own trial; but because it was a state, rather than a federal, case, he could not fall back on the Fifth Amendment right to avoid self-incrimination. Therefore, the prosecutor obtained a conviction by suggesting that the man's silence inferred his guilt. The Supreme Court had to decide whether the Fifth Amendment's protections applied to California through the due process clause of the Fourteenth Amendment. Although the high court upheld the man's conviction, four of the nine justices vehemently dissented, signaling the rising tide of support for total incorporation of fundamental rights under the due process clause. In the dissenting opinion, Justice Hugo L. Black wrote:

> My study of the historical events that culminated in the Fourteenth Amendment . . . persuades me that one of the chief objects that the provisions of the amendment's first section . . . were intended to accomplish was to make the Bill of Rights applicable to the states. . . . I would follow what I believe was the original purpose of the Fourteenth Amendment —to extend to all the people of the nation the complete protection of the Bill of Rights. To hold that this court can determine what, if any, provisions of the Bill of Rights will be enforced, and if so to what degree, is to frustrate the great design of a written Constitution.[4]

Thereafter, changing times and the advent, under Chief Justice Earl Warren (served 1953–1969), of a Supreme Court more responsive to the people's civil rights broke down the barriers against full incorporation of these rights into the due process clause. Between 1961 and 1969, the historic Warren Court at last defined the meaning of due process, including within it most of the rights outlined in the Fourth, Fifth, and Sixth Amendments. In 1961, the justices ruled that the full Fourth Amendment applied to the states through the due process clause of the Fourteenth Amendment (*Mapp v. Ohio*); in 1964, the Fifth Amendment self-incrimination clause was incorporated (*Malloy v. Hogan*); in 1965, the Sixth Amendment right of the accused to confront and cross-examine witnesses (*Pointer v. Texas*); in 1967, the right to a speedy trial (*Klopfer v. North Carolina*); and in 1969, the Fifth Amendment double jeopardy clause (*Benton v. Maryland*).

The overall result of this barrage of rulings, states noted law historian David Bodenhamer, "was a nationalized Bill of Rights that dimmed the local character of justice by applying the same restraints to all criminal proceedings, both state and federal."[5] The new complexion of this nationalized Bill of Rights strongly reflected Warren's personal philosophy that American law needed to be brought "more and more into harmony with moral principles." The pursuit of justice, he writes, is a process of continual revision of the cat-alogue of liberties, resulting "in a document that will not have exactly the same meaning it had when we received it from our fathers," but one even better because it has been "burnished by growing use."[6]

Earl Warren

Indeed, whatever the found-ers may have intended when they created the Bill of Rights, they surely did not mean it to be a legal straitjacket confining future generations to unbend-ing interpretation. They real-ized that new situations will inevitably call for new inter-pretations. And they would be grateful to the Warren Court for choosing the high moral path of more, rather than less, freedom.

1. John M. Harlan, *Hurtado v. California* (1884), quoted in William Dudley, ed., *The Bill of Rights: Opposing Viewpoints*. San Diego: Greenhaven Press, 1994, p. 209.

2. Joseph Hurtado was convicted of murder by the state of California and sentenced to be hanged. He claimed that he had been denied due process because California criminal law did not at that time provide for indictment by a grand jury in such cases, a guarantee of the Fifth Amendment.

3. Joel M. Gora, ed., *Due Process of Law*. Skokie, IL: National Textbook Company, 1977, p. 5.

4. Hugo L. Black, *Adamson v. California* (1947), quoted in Gora, *Due Process of Law*, p. 8.

5. David J. Bodenhamer, *Fair Trial: Rights of the Accused in American History*. New York: Oxford University Press, 1992, p. 113.

6. Earl Warren, "The Law and the Future," 1955, quoted in Bodenhamer, *Fair Trial*, p. 111.

"Due process is a fairly limited right rather than a broad general one. . . . A broad guarantee would have been singled out [by the Constitution's framers] as a separate amendment."

Due Process Need Not Include All Sections of the Bill of Rights

The phrase "due process of law," as it appears in the Fifth Amendment, has been a controversial one. Some scholars suggest that the clause in which the phrase appears should be interpreted in a very broad sense, to include not only the other clauses of that amendment, but virtually all other civil rights guarantees as well. The Warren Court (named after Chief Justice Earl Warren, who headed the Supreme Court from 1953 to 1969) certainly interpreted due process in a broad and liberal way. In a process of "selective incorporation" (already begun modestly in prior decades), the Warren Court redefined the meaning of the phrase.

That Court's justices decided, in effect, that due process is a criminal justice procedure guaranteeing the liberties listed in the Bill of Rights, particularly in Amendments Four, Five, and Six; and that this procedure should be applied in state and local, as well as federal, cases. Their method was to incorporate liberties from the Bill of Rights into the due process clause of the Fourteenth Amendment, passed in 1868. That amendment bars any state from depriving "any person of life, liberty, or property, without due process of law." By forcing state and local authorities to apply most of the provisions of the Bill of Rights to their own cases, the Court "nationalized" the Bill.

In doing so, however, these well-meaning but overly zealous and too liberal justices also distorted the original spirit and legal implications of the phrase "due process of law" as intended by the founders. The founders did not mean for that

Drawing by Handelsman; © 1970 The New Yorker Magazine, Inc.

"What's so great about due process? Due process got me ten years."

phrase to be all-inclusive; for if they had, they would have worded the Fifth Amendment differently. Christopher Wolfe, associate professor of political science at Marquette University, suggests considering the placement of the phrase in the amendment and the weight that placement gives it. He breaks down the provisions as follows:

> Amendment 5: Rules Governing Proceedings against Life, Liberty, and Property (applicable especially to pretrial matters)
> 1. Grand jury requirement;
> 2. Double jeopardy prohibition;
> 3. Self-incrimination prohibition, due process;
> 4. Just compensation requirement.[1]

Note that due process is placed in the second half of the third of the amendment's four sections, the separateness of each emphasized by the use of semicolons. "This placement . . . buried in the midst of a number of specific rights," concludes Wolfe,

> suggests rather strongly that due process is a fairly limited right rather than a broad general one. On its face, it makes quite unlikely the very broad form of procedural due process, according to which it is a general guarantee of fair or just legal process. Such a broad guarantee would have been singled out as a separate amendment (like trial by jury in civil cases [Amendment Seven]) or at least placed at the beginning or, more likely, the end of the procedural guaranties.[2]

If the original due process clause was not an all-inclusive grab bag of rights, then what was it? In the landmark 1884 *Hurtado v. California* case, Justice Stanley Matthews, speaking for the majority of his Supreme Court colleagues, defined it as the "law of the land." By this he meant the standing, common laws of the courts, derived mainly from the parent English legal system; so that a person's right to due process is the general guarantee of receiving a fair trial under the country's existing body of law, *not* a list of specific guarantees. Backing him on this point was the definition of his distinguished predecessor, Justice Joseph Story (served 1812–1845), who said that the due process clause "in effect affirms the right of trial according to the process of proceedings of the common law."[3] In summary, Matthews stated that due process

> refers to that law of the land, which derives its authority from the legislative powers conferred upon Congress by the Constitution of the United States . . . and interpreted according to the principles of the common law. In the 14th Amendment, by parity of reason, it refers to that law of the land of each state, which derives its authority from the inherent and reserved powers of the state, exerted within the limits of those fundamental principles of liberty and justice which lie at the base of all our civil and political institutions, and the greatest security for which resides in the right of the people to make their own laws, and alter them at their pleasure.[4]

The key phrase here is the "right of the people to make their own laws, and alter them." By this, Matthews means that the body of common law would naturally vary from state to state, since each state legislature has the right to enact, modify, or repeal laws at their leisure. The effect is that the federal body of law may differ from the individual state bodies of law. So, due process may have one result in a federal case and different results in various state cases; and an accused person might, for example, be entitled to a grand jury indictment in one state, but not in a neighboring state.

Thus, due process was originally intended in a rather narrow sense. It referred to the right of trial by common, or "prevailing law," in other words the laws of the courts as they are made or unmade by the state legislatures. By contrast, the core rights mentioned in the Bill of Rights were intended to be unchangeable. As for the appearance of the due process clause in the Fifth Amendment list of rights, as Wolfe puts it:

> It is as if the framers . . . were saying: "In addition to these specific rights we have mentioned, which are constitutionally guaranteed beyond legislative mod- ification, the other rules of legal proceedings in effect at a given time—whatever they may be—are also to be accorded persons before punishing them."[5]

If this original and correct interpretation of basic liberties, including due process, were still followed today, the United States would not be deluged by a virtual tidal wave of crime. The Warren Court went much too far in extending the defi- nition of due process to include so many basic rights. And this has, in the ensuing decades, made it increasingly difficult for law enforcement authorities to do their jobs and restrain criminals. Law historian David Bodenhamer summarizes what concerned citizens view as the ill effects of this distorted appli- cation of due process:

> According to this view, the Warren Court . . . aban- doned the discovery of truth, the traditional goal of American criminal procedure, in a misguided and unjustified expansion of defendants' rights. These rights enabled criminals to escape punishment—and worse, to continue a life of crime—not through a trial determination of guilt or innocence but rather on some technicality that bore little relationship to what actually happened.[6]

Our only hope to reduce significantly the incidence of crime and to restore order in a criminal justice system that is clearly *out of order* is to punish the guilty. Punishing criminals is, after all, the primary mission of that system. We cannot achieve this important goal, however, until the trial process regains its integrity and its central role in the system. Police and prosecu- tors must have the freedom to present evidence of guilt or innocence without being overly hampered by a barrage of rights that serious criminals claim through invoking a due process clause that originally did not accord them these rights.

1. Christopher Wolfe, "The Original Meaning of the Due Process Clause," in Eugene W. Hickok Jr., ed., *The Bill of Rights: Original Meaning and Current Understanding*. Charlottesville: University Press of Virginia, 1991, p. 218.

2. Wolfe, "The Original Meaning of the Due Process Clause," in Hickok, *The Bill of Rights*, pp. 218–19.

3. Joseph Story, *Commentaries on the Constitution of the United States*. Boston: Hilliard, Gray, 1833, section 1, 789.

4. Stanley Matthews, *Hurtado v. California* (1884), quoted in Joel M. Gora, ed., *Due Process of Law*. Skokie, IL: National Textbook Company, 1977, p. 4.

5. Wolfe, "The Original Meaning of the Due Process Clause," in Hickok, *The Bill of Rights*, p. 222.

6. David J. Bodenhamer, "Reversing the Revolution: Rights of the Accused in a Conservative Age," in David J. Bodenhamer and James W. Ely Jr., eds., *The Bill of Rights in Modern America After 200 Years*. Bloomington: Indiana University Press, 1993, pp. 101–102.

CHAPTER 4

Some Modern Challenges to the Bill of Rights

"The overwhelming urge to pay back the criminal—to avenge the victim and to exact the price of justice from the wrongdoer—is . . . a normal, healthy feeling . . . one that . . . makes us human and sets us apart from mere animals."

The Death Penalty Does Not Constitute Cruel and Unusual Punishment

The Eighth Amendment to the U.S. Constitution reads: "Excessive bail shall not be required, nor excessive fines imposed, nor cruel and unusual punishments inflicted." Regarding the last part, "cruel and unusual punishments" are not defined; nor is the death penalty mentioned at all. Clearly, the founders did not think that capital punishment is cruel and unusual, or else they would have inserted words to that effect in this section of the Bill of Rights. We should follow their wisdom. They knew that the death penalty is not cruel but justified for at least three reasons that still hold true today: first, that it is the people's will; second, that it is constitutional; and third, that it is morally compelling.

That the Eighth Amendment does not specify what punishments should be considered cruel and unusual is only fitting, for the people inevitably decide that for themselves. The amendment's brevity, generality, and lack of specific definitions have left it up to the courts—state, federal, and Supreme—as well as evolving social traditions and changing public opinion, to define cruel punishment. And indeed, of these arenas, the last—changing public opinion—has proven to be the most important. In 1791, when the Bill of Rights was ratified, such punishments as public whippings, branding with hot irons, and ear-cropping were common in the United States. Over the years such penalties were outlawed, but not because of court challenges to the Eighth Amendment. Instead, as Joseph L. Hoffman, a law professor at Indiana University at Bloomington, points out:

> Sentencing reform in this country has been driven by the moral judgment of the American people, as expressed in the statutory enactments of legislatures, the discretionary decisions of prosecutors, the verdicts of juries, and the sentencing pronouncements of trial judges. With few exceptions, whenever a majority of Americans have decided that a punishment is unacceptably "cruel and unusual" . . . no constitutional provision or reviewing court has been needed to fix the problem—the punishment has simply fallen into disuse, either because the authorization for it was revoked or because juries and trial judges no longer tolerated its imposition.[1]

The main point here is that, over the long run, the American people largely decide what punishments are acceptable; and throughout U.S. history, poll after poll has shown that a large majority of the public supports the death penalty for murder. The exact numbers vary from place to place and time to time, but an Associated Press poll taken in the late 1980s was fairly typical. It registered 86 percent for and only 11 percent against murderers receiving capital punishment. Clearly, those who argue that the death penalty is cruel are out of touch with the feelings of most of their neighbors.

As for the claim that capital punishment is unconstitutional because it violates the Eighth Amendment's bar against cruel and unusual punishments, the Supreme Court has said otherwise. In fact, very few cases applying the death penalty to the Eighth Amendment have ever reached the high court. In one of the first, *McGautha v. California* (1971), the Court wisely ruled that juries have the right to impose the death penalty completely at their own discretion and do not have to worry about upholding constitutional standards. "The states are entitled to assume," wrote Justice John M. Harlan, "that jurors confronted with the truly awesome responsibility of decreeing death for a fellow human will act with due regard to the consequences of their decision."[2]

Furman v. Georgia

In the more controversial decision of the following year, *Furman v. Georgia*, the justices acted a good deal less wisely. A slim majority of five of them ruled that the death penalty, as administered in the United States, was unconstitutional because decisions about who would live or die were too often made in an arbitrary, discriminatory, or "freakish" manner. As Hoffman puts it, "The challenge posed by such a ruling was daunting: how to explain to the American people that the death penalty was 'cruel and unusual,' when most people, or at least a substantial percentage of them, accepted the morality of the death penalty."[3]

In plain fact, the Court majority *could not* meet this challenge. Although the majority opinion, as expressed by Justices William Brennan and Thurgood Marshall, was very well and earnestly written, it did not satisfy the American public. A majority of Americans, along with most of their state and federal legislators, felt that the Supreme Court had become too soft on crime. The *Furman* ruling, says former Assistant Attorney General of the U.S. William B. Reynolds, "contained no coherent principle" and "served both the people and the Constitution poorly."[4] In contrast, the opinions of the Court's dissenters tended to resonate more with the public. One of them, Chief Justice Warren E. Burger, stated:

There are no obvious indications that capital punishment offends the conscience of society to such a degree that our traditional deference to the legislative judgment must be abandoned. It is not a punishment such as burning at the stake that everyone would ineffably find to be repugnant to all civilized standards. Nor is it a punishment so roundly condemned that only a few aberrant legislatures have retained it on the statute books. Capital punishment is authorized by statute in 40 states, the District of Columbia, and in the federal courts for the commission of certain crimes.[5]

Luckily, this argument was vindicated four years later in the landmark *Gregg v. Georgia* case. In the *Furman* case, the Court had ruled that the death penalty, *as administered*, was unconstitutional, not that it was unconstitutional *per se*, or in and of itself. Meeting this challenge, thirty-five states rather speedily revised their death penalty statutes in an attempt to satisfy the high court that they could administer that penalty fairly. The Court indeed seemed satisfied, declaring in a seven-to-two vote in *Gregg v. Georgia* that the death penalty *is* constitutional per se. This ruling has not met with any serious challenges since that time because the American public still overwhelmingly supports capital punishment.

The acceptance by the public and Supreme Court alike that the death penalty is not cruel but justified follows naturally from society's and humanity's moral principles. Perhaps no one has more eloquently stated this fact than William Reynolds:

In some instances, capital punishment is not only morally permissible but morally compelled: morally compelled, that is, if we believe that life has any moral content whatsoever . . . if we believe life has any purpose and meaning. . . . Some crimes take us beyond the purely unacceptable to a fundamental outrage that the basic norms of any civilized community have been irretrievably transgressed. Vicious, cold-blooded murder is such a crime. So is treason. . . . Such crimes arouse our most intense feelings. . . . The overwhelming urge to pay back the criminal—to avenge the victim and to exact the price of justice from the wrongdoer—is shared by most Americans. The fancy word for this is "retribution." It is a normal, healthy feeling, and one that, among others, makes us human and sets us apart from mere animals. . . . The desire . . . for retribution against those who criminally violate others in society is a positive individual and community response. Indifference to the criminal's fate is, by contrast, a sign of moral decay and decline.[6]

1. Joseph L. Hoffman, "The 'Cruel and Unusual Punishment' Clause: A Limit on the Power to Punish or Constitutional Rhetoric?" in David J. Bodenhamer and James W. Ely Jr., eds., *The Bill of Rights in Modern America After 200 Years*. Bloomington: Indiana University Press, 1993, pp. 139–40.

2. John M. Harlan, *McGautha v. California* (1971), quoted in Joel M. Gora, ed., *Due Process of Law*. Skokie, IL: National Textbook Company, 1977, p. 167. Justice Harlan, who died in 1971, was the grandson of his namesake, who served on the high court from 1877 to 1911.

3. Hoffman, "The 'Cruel and Unusual Punishment' Clause," in Bodenhamer and Ely, *The Bill of Rights*, p. 145.

4. William B. Reynolds, "The Death Penalty Is Not Cruel and Unusual Punishment," in Eugene W. Hickok Jr., ed., *The Bill of Rights: Original Meaning and Current Understanding*. Charlottesville: University Press of Virginia, 1991, p. 324.

5. Warren E. Burger, *Furman v. Georgia* (1972), quoted in Gora, *Due Process of Law*, p. 171.

6. Reynolds, "The Death Penalty Is Not Cruel and Unusual Punishment," in Hickok, *The Bill of Rights*, pp. 327–28.

"The cruelty of the death penalty is evident. Like torture, an execution constitutes an extreme physical and mental assault on a person already rendered helpless by government authorities."

The Death Penalty Constitutes Cruel and Unusual Punishment

The United States is the only Western democratic nation that retains the death penalty. Seventy-three countries have abolished it (fifteen of these retain it only in certain extraordinary circumstances, such as wartime); and the present rate of abolition is two nations per year. What realization have these nations come to that the United States, so far, has not? Simply put, those countries that have rid themselves of capital punishment realize that it is morally wrong, ineffective as a deterrent, and extremely cruel.

Let us focus here on the last of these indictments—cruelty. Almost all Americans who say they support the death penalty for murder and other serious crimes also claim they are squarely against torturing prisoners, an uncivilized practice that our nation has repudiated throughout its history. Death penalty advocates evidently have not stopped to consider that execution is, by its very nature, the most extreme form of torture. According to Amnesty International, the famous independent watchdog group that monitors human rights violations worldwide:

> There can never be a justification for torture or for cruel, inhuman or degrading treatment or punishment. The cruelty of the death penalty is evident. Like torture, an execution constitutes an extreme physical and mental assault on a person already rendered helpless by government authorities. If hanging a woman by her arms until she experiences excruciating pain is rightly condemned as torture, how does one describe hanging her by the neck until she is dead? If administering 100 volts of electricity to the most sensitive parts of a man's body evokes disgust, what is the appropriate reaction to the administration of 2,000 volts to his body in order to kill him? . . . Does the interpolation of legal process in these cruelties make their inhumanity justifiable? [1]

Following from this correlation of the death penalty with torture is the question of who should be an executioner? Some would say that it is the state that orders the execution and therefore that no individual is responsible for the actual killing of the condemned. But as one of the greatest trial lawyers this nation has ever produced, Clarence Darrow, asked, "How many men and women would be willing to act as executioners? How many fathers and mothers would want their children to witness an official killing?"[2] The answer to Darrow's first question is—very few; and to his second—none, even among those parents who strongly support capital punishment. But why, if a person is for the death penalty, should he or she be squeamish about taking an active role in enforcing it? Quite clearly, even the most vehement advocate of state executions finds the actual act of killing someone repugnant and barbaric, a deed better left to the "executioners," whomever they may be. Yet the sad fact is that when our country, in which the people *are* the state, uses the death penalty, we are all the executioners. As Darrow inquired:

> How can the state censure the cruelty of the man who . . . takes human life, when everyone knows that

the state itself, after long premeditation and settled hatred, not only kills, but first tortures and bedevils its victims for weeks [often months or years] with the impending doom?[3]

Indeed, the torture prisoners endure while waiting on death row is a prominent example of the cruelty of capital punishment. Noted defense attorney and death penalty opponent Robert R. Bryan states:

A person is placed on death row and told that he or she will be killed. The authorities plan it, there is a ceremony and procedure, and the damned sits there, year after year, continually reminded that "We are going to kill you—but not yet. This is how we are going to kill you—but not yet. We are going to electrocute you, or gas you, or give you a lethal injection—but not yet." It is the ultimate torture and barbaric treatment of a fellow human being.[4]

Still another factor that makes the death penalty cruel and unusual punishment is the very real possibility of unforeseen errors made by executioners or their equipment. Such mistakes can and have transformed what might have been relatively quick deaths into prolonged, agonizing affairs that would turn the stomach and plague the conscience of the strongest capital punishment advocate. The most famous example, of which many such advocates are blissfully unaware, occurred in 1947 in Louisiana. It led to *Louisiana v. Resweber*, the second ever Supreme Court review of the Eighth Amendment's cruel and unusual punishment clause. Constitutional historian Andrew Weinberger recalls the circumstances:

The petitioner was duly convicted in the Louisiana state courts of murder and sentenced to be electrocuted. . . . He was placed in the electric chair. The switch was thrown by the executioner but, because of some mechanical difficulty, death did not result even though some electricity passed through the prisoner. The Supreme Court, by a five to four decision, denied the appellant's claim that to subject him to a second attempt at execution was cruel and unusual punishment when tested against the Eighth Amendment.[5]

The vehement argument presented by the four dissenting judges stated in part:

> Taking human life by unnecessarily cruel means shocks the most fundamental instincts of civilized man. It should not be possible under the constitutional procedure of a self-governing people. Abhorrence of the cruelty of ancient forms of capital punishment has increased steadily until, today, some states have prohibited capital punishment altogether. It is unthinkable that any state legislature in modern times would enact a statute expressly authorizing . . . repeated applications of an electric current separated by intervals of days or hours until finally death shall result.[6]

Louisiana v. Resweber, in which the forces of reason and humanity narrowly lost, proved but a prelude to the historic *Furman v. Georgia* (1972), in which they won. The Court declared that arbitrary and "freakish" applications of the death penalty, as well as "evolving standards of decency," had rendered it unconstitutional. Justice William J. Brennan declared: "The state, even as it punishes, must treat its members with respect for their intrinsic worth as human beings. A punishment is 'cruel and unusual,' therefore, if it does not comport with human dignity."[7] Justice Thurgood Marshall concurred, saying:

> A penalty that was permissible at one time in our nation's history is not necessarily permissible today. . . . In striking down capital punishment, this Court does not malign our system of government. On the

Thurgood Marshall

contrary, it pays homage to it. Only in a free society . . . could civilization record its magnificent advancement. In recognizing the humanity of our fellow beings, we pay ourselves the highest tribute. We achieve "a major milestone in the long road up from barbarism," and join the approximately 70 other jurisdictions in the world which celebrate their regard for civilization and humanity by shunning capital punishment.[8]

Unfortunately, this landmark judgment was largely reversed four years later in *Gregg v. Georgia* and other cases that allowed the states to resume executing prisoners. In the face of these setbacks, concerned citizens must continue to lobby their senators and congresspersons for a return to the spirit of *Furman*. Only by speaking out for justice and humane treatment can we hope to see the coming of an age like that so eloquently envisioned by the great Clarence Darrow:

> The time will come when all people will view with horror the light way in which society and its courts of law now take human life; and when that time comes, the way will be clear to devise some better method of dealing with poverty and ignorance and their frequent by-products which we call crime.[9]

1. Amnesty International, *When the State Kills . . . The Death Penalty: A Human Rights Issue*. New York: Amnesty International, 1989, p. 2.

2. Clarence Darrow, "The Futility of the Death Penalty," 1928, in Carol Wekesser, ed., *The Death Penalty: Opposing Viewpoints*. San Diego: Greenhaven Press, 1991, p. 52.

3. Darrow, "The Futility of the Death Penalty," in Wekesser, *The Death Penalty*, p. 52.

4. Robert R. Bryan, "The Defender," in Ian Gray and Moira Stanley, eds., *A Punishment in Search of a Crime: Americans Speak Out Against the Death Penalty*. New York: Avon Books, 1989, p. 322.

5. Andrew D. Weinberger, *Freedom and Protection: The Bill of Rights*. San Francisco: Chandler Publishing, 1962, p. 83.

6. Harold H. Burton, with William O. Douglas, Frank Murphy, and Wiley B. Rutledge concurring, *Louisiana v. Resweber* (1947), quoted in Milton R. Konvitz, ed., *Bill of Rights Reader: Leading Constitutional Cases*. Ithaca, NY: Cornell University Press, 1960, p. 710.

7. William J. Brennan, *Furman v. Georgia* (1972), quoted in Joel M. Gora, ed., *Due Process of Law*. Skokie, IL: National Textbook Company, 1977, pp. 168–69.

8. Thurgood Marshall, *Furman v. Georgia*, quoted in Gora, *Due Process of Law*, pp. 170–71. The sections set off by quotation marks refer to opinions rendered in prior Supreme Court rulings.

9. Darrow, "The Futility of the Death Penalty," in Wekesser, *The Death Penalty*, p. 52.

"When under conditions of modern warfare our shores are threatened by hostile forces, the power to protect must be commensurate with the threatened danger."

War Justifies Restricting Civil Liberties

No thoughtful American likes the idea of imposing limits on citizens' civil rights. And under normal circumstances, no such limits should be imposed. However, war, especially all-out struggles for the country's survival such as the Civil War and World War II, produce circumstances that are far from normal. During such conflicts, the nation faces not only the threat of attack from the outside, but also the very real danger of assault from the inside; for spies, enemy agents, and those few American citizens who sympathize with the enemy inevitably attempt to undermine the war effort and thereby to bring about the defeat and destruction of the United States. Thus, under the special dangerous conditions that arise during wartime, we must, for the sake of our survival as a people, restrict some persons' civil liberties.

For example, such dangerous conditions and the country's need to protect itself were behind the passage of the Espionage Act in 1917 and its amendment, the 1918 Sedition Act. The former made it a crime for a person to obstruct military recruiting or to cause acts of subordination in the armed forces. These are perfectly reasonable restrictions that in the long run harm only those who want the country to lose the war, that is, its enemies. The Sedition Act went further, stating: "Whoever, when the United States is at war, shall willfully utter, print, write, or publish . . . any language intended to incite, provoke, or encourage resistance to the United States, or to promote the cause of its enemies . . . shall be punished."[1] This strongly worded law could, admittedly, have been misused by overzealous authorities to imprison innocent people. But this is the relatively small risk that a great nation such as ours must take in order to survive in times of ultimate crisis.

And anyway, no innocent persons *were* imprisoned under the Sedition Act. Those convicted had openly called for obstructing the war effort, and this made them, in effect, enemies of the country. What is more, both the Espionage and Sedition Acts were deemed constitutional by the Supreme Court. The Court upheld the Espionage Act in the 1919 *Frohwerk v. United States* case;[2] and in another case that same

Reprinted by permission of Steve Kelley.

year, *Abrams v. United States*, the justices found that the Sedition Act did not violate the Constitution. In question in *Abrams* was the distribution of antigovernment leaflets, one of which called for American workers to go on strike to stop the production of ammunition being used to "murder" both Germans and Russians. Speaking for the majority, Justice John H. Clarke wrote that the leaflets did not constitute "an attempt to bring about a change of [government] administration by candid discussion." Rather, Clarke stated, they were intended to "excite, at the supreme crisis of the war, disaffection, sedition, riots, and . . . revolution" in an attempt to bring about the defeat of the United States.[3]

Even more compelling than these arguments for restrictions of certain liberties during wartime were those of one of our greatest and most beloved national leaders. Abraham Lincoln is widely recognized not only as a courageous and effective president, but also as a staunch believer in human rights. Yet he faced the daunting task of keeping the nation from being torn asunder during the bloody Civil War; and he recognized that to achieve that goal, it would be necessary to place some limits on liberties that would be unwarranted in peacetime. Accordingly, he ordered thousands of suspected Confederate sympathizers arrested and detained, in the process suppressing some of their civil rights, including that of habeas corpus (the right of an accused person to be formally charged in court). Such strict measures were a "duty he could not forebear" as president, he said, and would do no serious harm to the Bill of Rights in the long run. In a letter to some citizens who had expressed concern about these measures, he stated:

> Ours is a case of rebellion . . . in fact, a clear, flagrant, and gigantic piece of rebellion; and the provision in the Constitution that "the privilege of the writ of habeas corpus shall not be suspended unless when, in cases of rebellion or invasion, the public safety may require it," is the provision which spe-

cially applies to our present case. This provision plainly attests the understanding of those who made the Constitution that ordinary courts of justice are inadequate to "cases of rebellion". . . . Habeas corpus does not discharge men who are proved to be guilty of defined crime; and its suspension is allowed by the Constitution on purpose that men may be arrested and held who cannot be proved to be guilty of defined crime, "when, in cases of rebellion or invasion, the public safety may require it." This is precisely our present case—a case of rebellion wherein the public safety does require the suspension. . . . I am [not] able to appreciate the danger apprehended . . . that the American people will by means of military arrests during the rebellion lose the right of public discussion [and other civil rights] throughout the indefinite peaceful future which I trust lies before them.[4]

Lincoln's promise that civil rights would be restored for everyone when the national crisis was over was fulfilled. In the peaceful decades that followed, the government did not become a tyranny, as many had feared it might.

Lincoln's handling of the Civil War also established important precedents for any dire crises the country might face in the future. The most dire of all, World War II, of course, brought the United States face-to-face with the greatest threat it or any other nation had yet seen—world domination by totalitarian regimes and the complete destruction of democracy.

Abraham Lincoln

Once again, the government faced the unwanted but necessary task of placing restrictions on some civil rights.

The most famous example was the temporary relocation, in 1942, of about one hundred thousand California residents of Japanese ancestry to small housing encampments guarded by military personnel. Some people have characterized this action as unfair and even racist. Yet at the time, military leaders had sufficient reasons to fear that some of those detained might be Japanese spies planning to help guide enemy ships and bombers to our shores. It was clearly a matter of temporarily sacrificing the comfort of a few for the lasting preservation of everyone. This was part of the reasoning used by the majority of Supreme Court justices who upheld the relocation action in *Korematsu v. United States* in 1944. Speaking for that majority, Justice Hugo L. Black declared:

> Hardships are a part of war and war is an aggregation [collection] of hardships. All citizens alike, both in and out of uniform, feel the impact of war in greater or lesser measure. Citizenship has its responsibilities as well as its privileges, and in time of war the burden is always heavier. Compulsory exclusion of large groups of citizens from their homes, except under circumstances of direst emergency and peril, is inconsistent with our basic governmental institutions. But when under conditions of modern warfare our shores are threatened by hostile forces, the power to protect must be commensurate with the threatened danger. . . . There was evidence of disloyalty on the part of some [of those Japanese who were relocated], the military authorities considered that the need for action was great, and time was short. We cannot—by availing ourselves of the calm perspective of hindsight—now say that at that time these actions were unjustified.[5]

Indeed, it is too easy to sit back today, in peacetime, with the United States secure in its status as the world's great superpower, and smugly to say that this or that action taken half a century ago was wrong. In the midst of the ultimate crisis the country faced in the most terrible war in history, military and government authorities fulfilled their sworn duty to protect the country at all costs.

1. See Appendix A for a more detailed quotation from the Sedition Act's text.

2. The case involved the conviction of a man who had published, in a German-language newspaper, articles saying that both World War I and U.S. military conscription for that conflict were unconstitutional.

3. John H. Clarke, *Abrams v. United States* (1919), quoted in Lucius J. Barker and Twiley W. Barker Jr., eds., *Civil Liberties and the Constitution: Cases and Commentaries.* Englewood Cliffs, NJ: Prentice-Hall, 1975, pp. 173–74.

4. Abraham Lincoln, "Letter of June 12, 1863, to Erastus Corning and Others," in Roy P. Basler, ed., *Abraham Lincoln: His Speeches and Writings.* Cleveland: World Publishing, 1946, pp. 702, 705.

5. Hugo L. Black, *Korematsu v. United States* (1944), quoted in William Dudley, ed., *The Bill of Rights: Opposing Viewpoints.* San Diego: Greenhaven Press, 1994, pp. 175–76.

"The Constitution of the United States is a law for rulers and people, equally in war and peace, and covers with the shield of its protection all classes of men, at all times, and under all circumstances."

Wartime National Security Does Not Justify Restricting Civil Liberties

It is during the crisis of war that a democracy like the United States finds its commitment to personal freedoms most severely tested. There are bound to be some citizens who disagree with how the government conducts a particular war effort, or, as in the case of Vietnam, with the need for the country to be involved at all. Such protesters have as much right to speak their mind about national policy in wartime as they do in peacetime; and silencing them only allows the government to set an ominous precedent of restricting civil liberties for everyone whenever a handful of public officials deems it appropriate.

Even more ominous than silencing protesters is suppressing the liberties of those who have said or done nothing at all but whom the government thinks constitute a "potential threat" to national security. It is one thing to detain a person who has committed an overt criminal violation and quite another to confine someone who "might" do so in the future. Yet the government has on a number of occasions illegally detained thousands of citizens, suspending their rights to trial or of confronting the witnesses against them.

One of these occasions was during the Civil War when President Lincoln ordered many Northerners suspected of being "Confederate sympathizers" arrested and held without recourse to most of the guarantees of the Bill of Rights. Openly admitting that those imprisoned had committed no crimes, Lincoln used the excuse that the government does not have to follow normal legal procedures in the case of a rebellion. "Arrests by process of courts and arrests in cases of rebellion do not proceed altogether upon the same basis," he wrote.

> In the latter case arrests are made not so much for what has been done, as for what probably would be done. . . . The man who stands by and says nothing when the peril of his government is discussed, cannot be misunderstood. If not hindered, he is sure to help the enemy.[1]

Yet this is false and deceptive reasoning. Standing by and saying nothing while others verbally protest a war or criticize the government's handling of it is neither a crime nor a potential threat. And neither is the actual protest itself, according to the Bill of Rights. The Supreme Court unanimously said so a year after the end of the Civil War in reviewing the case of an Indiana man arrested for conspiring to help the enemy. Justice David Davis wrote:

> The Constitution of the United States is a law for rulers and people, equally in war and peace, and covers with the shield of its protection all classes of men, at all times, and under all circumstances. No doctrine involving more pernicious consequences, was ever invented by the wit of man than that any of its provisions can be suspended during any of the great exi-

gencies [immediate needs] of government. Such a doctrine leads directly to anarchy or despotism.[2]

Despite the high court's fair and legally sound ruling on the matter, Lincoln's suspension of liberties set a potentially dangerous precedent. The government later exploited this precedent in what proved to be the most flagrant case of its kind in the nation's history—the wrongful internment of Japanese Americans in the early years of World War II. At the time that the United States declared war on Japan (December 8, 1941), more than a hundred thousand Japanese, two-thirds of them American citizens, lived in western states, principally California. Fearing that they might aid the enemy by spying or by guiding invasion forces to selected American targets, the U.S. military wangled an executive order from President Franklin Roosevelt authorizing that Japanese Americans be evacuated from their homes and interned in other states. The announcement of the evacuation came on March 2, 1942; and in the next few months, over 117,000 people were relocated to detention camps guarded by armed troops.

It must be emphasized that none of those physically forced to leave their homes had done anything to indicate they were a threat to national security. After hundreds of FBI agents raided their neighborhoods looking for evidence that they were disloyal, U.S. Attorney General Francis Biddle admitted to President Roosevelt:

> We have not uncovered through these searches any dangerous persons that we could not otherwise know about. We have not found . . . any evidence . . . [of any] bombs . . . nor have we found any gun in any circumstances indicating that it was to be used in a manner helpful to our enemies. We have not found a camera which we have reason to believe was for use in espionage.[3]

This lack of evidence did not stop the implementation of the evacuation order, however. The reason that this travesty of justice continued was plainly a combination of hysteria and racism on the part of the authorities, the media, and large segments of the general public. Many agreed with popular newspaper columnist Henry McLemore when he wrote:

> I am for the immediate removal of every Japanese on the West Coast to a point deep in the interior. . . . Herd 'em up, pack 'em off and give them the inside room in the Badlands. Let 'em be pinched, hurt, hungry and dead up against it. . . . Let us have no patience with the enemy or with anyone whose veins carry his blood.[4]

Apprehensive youngsters arrive at a detention center following President Roosevelt's order to relocate and detain Japanese Americans during World War II.

The racist venom of Lieutenant General John L. De Witt, the man in charge of the defense of the West Coast, was even worse. "A Jap's a Jap," he replied to the internees' protests that they were loyal American citizens.

> They are a dangerous element. . . . There is no way to determine their loyalty. . . . It makes no difference if he [an internee] is an American; theoretically he is still Japanese, and you can't change him . . . by giving him a piece of paper.[5]

If De Witt was right, why, then, could "giving a piece of paper" to a German American or Italian American "change" him or her into a loyal citizen? The United States was at war with Germany and Italy as well as Japan. Why were German Americans and Italian Americans not rounded up and placed in camps? The answer is obvious: They were white, whereas Japanese Americans had the wrong skin tone and eye shape. Justice Frank Murphy concisely summed up the injustice of the situation in writing the dissenting opinion in the 1944 *Korematsu v. United States* case.[6] The reasons for the government's action, he said, appear

> to be largely an accumulation of much of the misinformation, half-truths and insinuations that for years have been directed against Japanese Americans by people with racial and economic prejudices—the same people who have been among the foremost advocates of the evacuation. . . . No adequate reason is given [by the government] for the failure to treat these Japanese Americans on an individual basis by holding investigations . . . to separate the loyal from the disloyal, as was done in the case of [some] persons of German and Italian ancestry. . . . Nor is there any denial of the fact that not one person of Japanese ancestry was accused or convicted of espionage or sabotage after Pearl Harbor while they were still free, a fact which is some evidence of the loyalty of the vast majority of these individuals. . . . I dissent,

therefore, from this legalization of racism. Racial discrimination in any form and in any degree has no justifiable part whatever in our democratic way of life.[7]

Murphy's courageous words were finally vindicated in 1988, when the U.S. government agreed to apologize for its mistake and to pay reparations to the survivors of the relocation.[8] Hopefully, the country has learned a hard lesson about the need to maintain everyone's rights under all conditions, even those of wartime. But there are no guarantees that it will not happen again; and so, we must remain ever vigilant in guarding the integrity of the nation's greatest asset, the Bill of Rights.

1. Abraham Lincoln, "Letter of June 12, 1863, to Erastus Corning and Others," in Roy P. Basler, ed., *Abraham Lincoln: His Speeches and Writings*. Cleveland: World Publishing, 1946, pp. 702–703.

2. David Davis, *Ex Parte Mulligan* (1866), quoted in William Dudley, ed., *The Bill of Rights: Opposing Viewpoints*. San Diego: Greenhaven Press, 1994, p. 168.

3. Quoted in Daniel S. Davis, *Behind the Barbed Wire: The Imprisonment of Japanese Americans During World War II*. New York: E.P. Dutton, 1982, p. 30.

4. Quoted in Davis, *Behind the Barbed Wire*, p. 33.

5. Quoted in Davis, *Behind the Barbed Wire*, p. 29.

6. The case involved a California shipyard worker named Fred Korematsu who challenged the legality of the relocation order.

7. Frank Murphy, *Korematsu v. United States* (1944), quoted in Dudley, *The Bill of Rights*, pp. 180–81.

8. Congress established the Commission on Wartime Relocation and Internment of Civilians in 1980 to investigate the World War II detention of Japanese Americans. CWRIC concluded that the cause had been "race prejudice, war hysteria, and a failure of political leadership" and recommended a payment of $20,000 to each internee. In 1988 CWRIC's recommendations became law, and in 1990 President George Bush apologized, saying in part, "A monetary sum and words alone cannot restore lost years or erase painful memories. . . . We can never fully right the wrongs of the past. But we can take a clear stand . . . and recognize that serious injustices were done." (Quoted from Jerry Stanley, *I Am an American: A True Story of Japanese Internment*. New York: Crown Publishers, 1994, p. 90.)

APPENDIX A

Excerpts from Original Documents Pertaining to the Bill of Rights

Editor's Note: The eleven documents are listed in chronological order of their composition.

Document 1: The English Bill of Rights

Presented by Parliament and agreed to by King William III and Queen Mary in 1689, the English Bill of Rights guaranteed the English people many civil liberties. Among the document's most important provisions were those forbidding the king from keeping a standing army or imposing taxes without the permission of Parliament. Some of the Bill's provisions were:

1. That the pretended power of suspending of laws or the execution of laws by regal authority without consent of Parliament is illegal.

2. That the pretended power of dispensing with laws . . . as it hath been assumed . . . of late, is illegal. . . .

4. That levying money for or to the use of the Crown . . . without grant of Parliament . . . is illegal.

5. That it is the right of the subject to petition [seek justice from] the king. . . .

6. That the raising or keeping of a standing army within the kingdom in time of peace, unless it be with consent of Parliament, is against the law. . . .

8. That elections of members of Parliament ought to be free.

9. That the freedom of speech, and debates or proceedings of Parliament, ought not to be impeached or questioned in any court or place out of Parliament.

10. That excessive bail [for those accused of crimes] ought not be required, nor excessive fines imposed; nor cruel and unusual punishment inflicted. . . .

12. That all grants and promises of fines and forfeitures [seizure of properties] of particular persons before conviction are illegal and void.

13. And that for redress of all grievances, and for the amending, strengthening, and preserving of the laws, Parliaments ought to be held frequently.

Don Nardo, *Democracy*. San Diego: Lucent Books, 1994, p. 111.

Document 2: The Virginia Bill of Rights

Following are some of the articles of the Virginia Bill of Rights, the first such document in the American colonies. It was substantially written by George Mason, and the state legislature adopted it on June 12, 1776.

1. That all men are by nature equally free and independent, and have certain inherent rights, of which, when they enter into a state of society, they cannot, by any compact, deprive or divest their posterity; namely, the

enjoyment of life and liberty, with the means of acquiring and possessing property, and pursuing and obtaining happiness and safety.

2. That all power is vested in, and consequently derived from, the people; that magistrates are their trustees and servants, and at all times amenable to them.

3. That government is, or ought to be, instituted for the common benefit, protection, and security, of the people, nation, or community; of all the various modes and forms of government that is best, which is capable of producing the greatest degree of happiness and safety, and is most effectually secured against the danger of maladministration; and that whenever any government shall be found inadequate or contrary to these purposes, a majority of the community hath an indubitable, unalienable, and indefeasible right, to reform, alter, or abolish it, in such manner as shall be judged most conducive to the publick weal. . . .

6. That elections of members to serve as representatives of the people, in assembly, ought to be free; and that all men, having sufficient evidence of permanent common interest with, and attachment to, the community, have the right of suffrage, and cannot be taxed or deprived of their property for publick uses without their own consent, or that of their representatives so elected, nor bound by any law to which they have not, in like manner, assented, for the publick good. . . .

8. That in all capital or criminal prosecutions a man hath a right to demand the cause and nature of his accusation, to be confronted with the accusers and witnesses, to call for evidence in his favour, and to a speedy trial by an impartial jury of his vicinage, without whose unanimous consent he cannot be found guilty, nor can he be compelled to give evidence against himself; that no man be deprived of his liberty except by the law of the land, or the judgment of his peers.

9. That excessive bail ought not to be required, nor excessive fines imposed, nor cruel and unusual punishments inflicted.

10. That general warrants, whereby any officer or messenger may be commanded to search suspected places without evidence of a fact committed, or to seize any person or persons not named, or whose offence is not particularly described and supported by evidence, are grievous and oppressive, and ought not to be granted. . . .

12. That the freedom of the press is one of the great bulwarks of liberty, and can never be restrained but by despotick governments.

13. That a well regulated militia, composed of the body of the people, trained to arms, is the proper, natural, and safe defence of a free state; that standing armies, in time of peace, should be avoided, as dangerous to liberty; and that, in all cases, the military should be under strict subordination to, and governed by, the civil power. . . .

16. That religion, or the duty which we owe to our CREATOR, and the manner of discharging it, can be directed only by reason and conviction, not by force or violence; and therefore all men are equally entitled to the free exercise of religion, according to the dictates of conscience; and that

it is the mutual duty of all to practice Christian forbearance, love, and charity, towards each other.

Edward Dumbauld, *The Bill of Rights and What It Means Today*. Westport, CT: Greenwood Press, 1979, p. 170.

Document 3: Hamilton's Objections to a Bill of Rights

Alexander Hamilton was one of the authors of the Federalist Papers, *published in 1788, which called for ratifying the new Constitution. In this excerpt from the well-known eighty-fourth paper, Hamilton explains why he thinks the nation needs no bill of rights.*

It has been several times truly remarked, that bills of rights are in their origin, stipulations between kings and their subjects, abridgments of prerogative in favor of privilege, reservations of rights not surrendered to the prince. Such was Magna Charta, obtained by the Barons, sword in hand, from king John. . . . Such also was the declaration of right presented by the lords and commons to the prince of Orange in 1688, and afterwards thrown into the form of an act of parliament, called the bill of rights. It is evident, therefore, that according to their primitive signification, they have no application to constitutions professedly founded upon the power of the people, and executed by their immediate representatives and servants. Here, in strictness, the people surrender nothing, and as they retain every thing, they have no need of particular reservations. "We the people of the United States, to secure the blessings of liberty to ourselves and our posterity, do ordain and establish this constitution for the United States of America." Here is a better recognition of popular rights than volumes of those aphorisms which make the principal figure in several of our state bills of rights, and which would sound much better in a treatise of ethics than in a constitution of government. . . .

I go further, and affirm that bills of rights, in the sense and in the extent in which they are contended for, are not only unnecessary in the proposed constitution, but would even be dangerous. They would contain various exceptions to powers which are not granted; and on this very account, would afford a colourable pretext to claim more than were granted. For why declare that things shall not be done which there is no power to do? Why for instance, should it be said, that the liberty of the press shall not be restrained, when no power is given by which restrictions may be imposed? I will not contend that such a provision would confer a regulating power; but it is evident that it would furnish, to men disposed to usurp, a plausible pretence for claiming that power. They might urge with a semblance of reason, that the constitution ought not to be charged with the absurdity of providing against the abuse of an authority, which was not given, and that the provision against restraining the liberty of the press afforded a clear implication, that a power to prescribe proper regulations concerning it, was intended to be vested in the national government. This may serve as a specimen of the numerous handles which would be given to the doctrine of constructive powers, by the indulgence of an injudicious zeal for bills of rights.

On the subject of the liberty of the press, as much has been said, I cannot forbear adding a remark or two: In the first place, I observe that there is not a syllable concerning it in the constitution of this state, and in the next, I contend that whatever has been said about it in that of any other state, amounts to nothing. What signifies a declaration that "the liberty of the press shall be inviolably preserved?" What is the liberty of the press? Who can give it any definition which would not leave the utmost latitude for evasion? I hold it to be impracticable; and from this, I infer, that its security, whatever fine declarations may be inserted in any constitution respecting it, must altogether depend on public opinion, and on the general spirit of the people and of the government. And here, after all, as intimated upon another occasion, must we seek for the only solid basis of all our rights.

Alexander Hamilton, *The Federalist, No. 84*, quoted in William Dudley, ed., *The Bill of Rights: Opposing Viewpoints*. San Diego: Greenhaven Press, 1994, pp. 38–40.

Document 4: Jefferson Advocates a Bill of Rights

In these excerpts from his letter of March 15, 1789, to his colleague James Madison, Thomas Jefferson reasons that even a bill of rights that proves only moderately effective will be better than none at all.

Your thoughts on the subject of the declaration of rights, in the letter of October the 17th, I have weighed with great satisfaction. Some of them had not occurred to me before but were acknowledged just in the moment they were presented to my mind. In the arguments in favor of a declaration of rights, you omit one which has great weight with me; the legal check which it puts into the hands of the judiciary. This is a body, which, if rendered independent and kept strictly to their own department, merits great confidence for their learning and integrity. . . . I am happy to find that, on the whole, you are a friend to this amendment. The declaration of rights is, like all other human blessings, alloyed with some inconveniences, and not accomplishing fully its object. But the good in this instance, vastly overweighs the evil. I cannot refrain from making short answers to the objections which your letter states to have been raised. 1. That the rights in question are reserved, by the manner in which the federal powers are granted. Answer. A constitutive act may, certainly, be so formed, as to need no declaration of rights. The act itself has the force of a declaration, as far as it goes, and if it goes to all material points, nothing more is wanting. In the draught of a constitution which I had once a thought of proposing in Virginia, and printed afterwards, I endeavored to reach all the great objects of public liberty, and did not mean to add a declaration of rights. Probably the object was imperfectly executed; but the deficiencies would have been supplied by others, in the course of discussion. But in a constitutive act which leaves some precious articles unnoticed, and raises implications against others, a declaration of rights becomes necessary, by way of supplement. . . . 2. A positive declaration of some essential rights could not be obtained in the requisite latitude. Answer. Half a loaf is better than no bread. If we cannot secure all our rights, let us secure what we can. 3. The limited powers of the federal government, and jealousy of the subordinate governments, afford a security which exists in no other instance. Answer. The first member of this seems resolvable into the first objection before stated. The jealousy of the subordinate governments is a precious reliance. But observe that those governments are only agents. They must have principles furnished them, whereon to found their opposition. The declaration of rights will be the text, whereby they will try all the acts of the federal government. In this view, it is necessary to the federal government also; as by the same text, they may try the opposition of the subordinate governments. 4. Experience proves the inefficacy of a bill of rights. True. But though it is not absolutely efficacious under all circumstances, it is of great potency always, and rarely inefficacious. A brace the more will often keep up the building which would have fallen, with that brace the less. . . .

Adrienne Koch and William Peden, eds., *The Life and Selected Writings of Thomas Jefferson*. New York: Random House, 1944, pp. 462–63.

Document 5: The U.S. Bill of Rights

This is the final version of the Bill of Rights, authored principally by James Madison and George Mason and ratified by the states in 1791.

Amendment I

Congress shall make no law respecting an establishment of religion, or prohibiting the free exercise thereof; or abridging the freedom of speech, or of the press; or the right of the people peaceably to assemble, and to petition the Government for a redress of grievances.

Amendment II

A well regulated Militia, being necessary to the security of a free State, the right of the people to keep and bear Arms, shall not be infringed.

Amendment III

No Soldier shall, in time of peace be quartered in any house, without the consent of the Owner, nor in time of war, but in a manner to be prescribed by law.

Amendment IV

The right of the people to be secure in their persons, houses, papers, and effects, against unreasonable searches and seizures, shall not be violated, and no Warrants shall issue, but upon probable cause, supported by Oath or affirmation, and particularly describing the place to be searched, and the persons or things to be seized.

Amendment V

No person shall be held to answer for a capital, or otherwise infamous crime, unless on a presentment or indictment of a Grand Jury, except in cases arising in the land or naval forces, or in the Militia, when in actual service in time of War or public danger; nor shall any person be subject for the same offence to be twice put in jeopardy of life or limb; nor shall be compelled in any criminal case to be a witness against himself, nor be deprived of life, liberty, or property, without due process of law; nor shall private property be taken for public use, without just compensation.

Amendment VI

In all criminal prosecutions, the accused shall enjoy the right to a speedy and public trial, by an impartial jury of the State and district wherein the crime shall have been committed, which district shall have been previously ascertained by law, and to be informed of the nature and cause of the accusation; to be confronted with the witnesses against him; to have compulsory process for obtaining witnesses in his favor, and to have the Assistance of Counsel for his defence.

Amendment VII

In Suits at common law, where the value in controversy shall exceed twenty dollars, the right of trial by jury shall be preserved, and no fact tried by a jury, shall be otherwise re-examined in any Court of the United States, than according to the rules of the common law.

Amendment VIII

Excessive bail shall not be required, nor excessive fines imposed, nor cruel and unusual punishments inflicted.

Amendment IX

The enumeration in the Constitution, of certain rights, shall not be construed to deny or disparage others retained by the people.

Amendment X

The powers not delegated to the United States by the Constitution, nor prohibited by it to the States, are reserved to the States respectively, or to the people.

William Dudley, ed., *The Creation of the Constitution: Opposing Viewpoints*. San Diego: Greenhaven Press, 1995, p. 290.

Document 6: Lincoln Defends His Restrictions of Civil Liberties

In this excerpt from his letter of June 12, 1863, to a group of citizens concerned about the government's detention of suspected enemy sympathizers, Abraham Lincoln contends that his actions are necessary for the nation's preservation.

Ours is a case of rebellion—so called by the resolutions before me—in fact, a clear, flagrant, and gigantic case of rebellion; and the provision of the Constitution that "the privilege of the writ of habeas corpus shall not be suspended unless when, in cases of rebellion or invasion, the public safety may require it," is the provision which specially applies to our present case. This provision plainly attests the understanding of those who made the Constitution that ordinary courts of justice are inadequate to "cases of rebellion"—attests their purpose that, in such cases, men may be held in custody whom the courts, acting on ordinary rules, would discharge. Habeas corpus does not discharge men who are proved to be guilty of defined crime; and its suspension is allowed by the Constitution on purpose that men may be arrested and held who cannot be proved to be guilty of defined crime, "when, in cases of rebellion or invasion, the public safety may require it."

This is precisely our present case—a case of rebellion wherein the public safety does require the suspension. Indeed, arrests by process of courts and arrests in cases of rebellion do not proceed altogether upon the same basis. The former is directed at the small percentage of ordinary and continuous perpetration of crime, while the latter is directed at sudden and extensive uprisings against the government, which, at most, will succeed or fail in no great length of time. In the latter case arrests are made not so much for what has been done, as for what probably would be done. The latter is more for the preventive and less for the vindictive than the former. In such cases the purposes of men are much more easily understood than in cases of ordinary crime. The man who stands by and says nothing when the peril of his government is discussed, cannot be misunderstood. If not hindered, he is sure to help the enemy; much more if he talks ambiguously—talks for his country with "buts," and "ifs" and "ands." Of how little value the constitutional provision I have quoted will be rendered if arrests shall never be made until defined crimes shall have been committed, may be illustrated by a few notable examples: General John C. Breckinridge, General Robert E. Lee, General Joseph E. Johnston, General John B. Magruder, General William B. Preston, General Simon B. Buckner, and Commodore Franklin Buchanan, now occupying the very highest places in the rebel war service, were all within the power of the government since the rebellion began, and were nearly as well known to be traitors then as now. Unquestionably if we had seized and held them, the insurgent cause would be much weaker. But no one of them had then committed any crime defined in the law. Every one of them, if arrested, would have been discharged on habeas corpus were the writ allowed to operate. In view of these and similar cases, I think the time not unlikely to come when I shall be blamed for having made too few arrests rather than too many. . . .

I can no more be persuaded that the government can constitutionally take no strong measures in time of rebellion, because it can be shown that the same could not be lawfully taken in time of peace, than I can be persuaded that a particular drug is not good medicine for a sick man because it can be shown to not be good food for a well one. Nor am I able to appreciate the danger apprehended by the meeting, that the American people will by means of military arrests during the rebellion lose the right of public discussion, the liberty of speech and the press, the law of evidence, trial by jury, and habeas corpus throughout the indefinite peaceful future which I trust lies before them, any more than I am able to believe that a man could contract so strong an appetite for emetics during temporary illness as to persist in feeding upon them during the remainder of his healthful life.

Roy P. Basler, ed., *Abraham Lincoln: His Speeches and Writings*. Cleveland: World Publishing, 1946, pp. 702–703, 705.

Document 7: The 1918 Sedition Act

Congress passed the Sedition Act, an amendment to the 1917 Espionage Act, in 1918 and repealed it in 1920. These excerpts exemplify the law's restrictive language, which many people saw as an illegal abridgment of the guarantees of the Bill of Rights.

Whoever, when the United States is at war, shall willfully utter, print, write, or publish any disloyal, profane, scurrilous, or abusive language about the form of government of the United States, or the military or naval forces of the United States, or the flag of the United States, or the uniform of the Army or Navy of the United States, or any language intended to bring the form of government of the United States, or the Constitution of the United States, or the military or naval forces of the United States, into contempt, scorn, contumely or disrepute, or shall willfully utter, print, write, or publish any language intended to incite, provoke, or encourage resistance to the United States, or to promote the cause of its enemies, . . . or shall willfully by utterance, writing, printing, publication, or language spoken, urge, incite, or advocate any curtailment of production in this country of anything or things, product or products, necessary or essential to the prosecution of the war in which the United States may be engaged, with intent by such curtailment to cripple or hinder the United States in the prosecution of the war . . . shall be punished by a fine of not more than $10,000 or imprisonment for not more than twenty years, or both.

William Dudley, ed., *The Bill of Rights: Opposing Viewpoints.* San Diego: Greenhaven Press, 1994, p. 80.

Document 8: Justice Holmes Establishes the "Clear and Present Danger" Doctrine

This is part of the majority opinion, written by Justice Oliver W. Holmes, in the landmark 1919 Schenck v. United States *case. In upholding Schenck's conviction, the Supreme Court said, in effect, that the First Amendment does not apply in cases where a "clear and present danger" threatens the public welfare.*

This is an indictment in three counts. The first charges a conspiracy to violate the Espionage Act of June 15, 1917 . . . by causing and attempting to cause insubordination, &c., in the military and naval forces of the United States, and to obstruct the recruiting and enlistment service of the United States, when the United States was at war with the German Empire, to-wit, that the defendants wilfully conspired to have printed and circulated to men who had been called and accepted for military service . . . a document set forth and alleged to be calculated to cause such insubordination and obstruction. The count alleges overt acts in pursuance of the conspiracy, ending in the distribution of the document set forth.

The second count alleges a conspiracy to commit an offense against the United States, to-wit, to use the mails for transmission of matter declared to be non-mailable by Title XII, § 2, of the Act of June 15, 1917, to-wit, the above-mentioned document. . . . The third count charges an unlawful use of the mails for the transmission of the same matter and otherwise as above. . . .

It is argued that the evidence, if admissible, was not sufficient to prove that the defendant Schenck was concerned in sending the documents. According to the testimony Schenck said he was general secretary of the Socialist Party and had charge of the Socialist headquarters from which the documents were sent. He identified a book found there as the minutes of the Executive Committee of the party. The book showed a resolution of August 13, 1917, that fifteen thousand leaflets should be printed on the other side of one of them in use, to be mailed to men who had passed exemption boards, and for distribution. . . .

The document in question upon its first printed side recited the first section of the Thirteenth Amendment, said that the idea embodied in it was violated by the Conscription Act and that a conscript is little better than a convict. In impassioned language it intimated that conscription was despotism in its worst form and a monstrous wrong against humanity in the interest of Wall Street's chosen few. It said, "Do not submit to intimidation," but in form at least confined itself to peaceful measures such as a petition for the repeal of the Act.

The other and later printed side of the sheet was headed, "Assert Your Rights." It stated reasons for alleging that anyone violated the Constitution when he refused to recognize "your right to assert your Opposition to the draft," and went on, "If you do not assert and support your rights, you are helping to deny or disparage rights which it is the solemn duty of all citizens and residents of the United States to retain." It described the arguments on the other side as coming from cunning politicians and a mercenary capitalist press, and even silent assent to the conscription law as helping to support an infamous conspiracy. It denied the power to send our citizens away to foreign shores to shoot up the people of other lands, and added that words could not express the condemnation such cold-blooded ruthlessness deserves, &c., winding up, "You must do your share to maintain, support and uphold the rights of the people of this country." Of course the document would not have been sent unless it had been intended to have some effect, and we do not see what effect it could be expected to have upon persons subject to the draft except to influence them to obstruct the carrying of it out. The defendants do not deny that the jury might find against them on this point.

But it is said, suppose that that was the tendency of this circular, it is protected by the First Amendment to the Constitution. . . .

We admit that in many places and in ordinary times the defendants in saying all that was said in the circular would have been within their constitutional rights. But the character of every act depends upon the circumstances in which it is done. . . . The most stringent protection of free speech would not protect a man in falsely shouting fire in a theater and causing a panic. It does not even protect a man from an injunction against uttering words that may have all the effect of force. . . . The question in every case is whether the words used are used in such circumstances and are of such a nature as to create a clear and present danger that they will bring about the substantive evils that Congress has a right to prevent. It is a question of proximity and degree.

When a nation is at war many things that might be said in time of peace are such a hindrance to its effort that their utterance will not be endured so long as men fight and that no court could regard them as protected by any constitutional right. . . .

William Dudley, ed., *The Bill of Rights: Opposing Viewpoints*. San Diego: Greenhaven Press, 1994, pp. 75–77.

Document 9: The Japanese Relocation Characterized as Racist

In these excerpts from his dissenting opinion in Korematsu v. United States *(1944), Justice Frank Murphy minces no words in condemning the government's internment of Japanese Americans during World War II, saying the action was motivated by fear and prejudice.*

This exclusion of "all persons of Japanese ancestry, both alien and non-alien," from the Pacific Coast area on a plea of military necessity in the absence of martial law ought not to be approved. Such exclusion goes over "the very brink of constitutional power" and falls into the ugly abyss of racism. . . .

It must be conceded that the military and naval situation in the spring of 1942 was such as to generate a very real fear of invasion of the Pacific Coast, accompanied by fears of sabotage and espionage in that area. The military command was therefore justified in adopting all reasonable means necessary to combat these dangers. In adjudging the military action taken in light of the then apparent dangers, we must not erect too high or too meticulous standards; it is necessary only that the action have some reasonable relation to the removal of the dangers of invasion, sabotage and espionage. But the exclusion, either temporarily or permanently, of all persons with Japanese blood in their veins has no such reasonable relation. And that relation is lacking because the exclusion order necessarily must rely for its reasonableness upon the assumption that *all* persons of Japanese ancestry may have a dangerous tendency to commit sabotage and espionage and to aid our Japanese enemy in other ways. It is difficult to believe that reason, logic or experience could be marshalled in support of such an assumption. . . .

The main reasons relied upon by those responsible for the forced evacuation, therefore, do not prove a reasonable relation between the group characteristics of Japanese Americans and the dangers of invasion, sabotage and espionage. The reasons appear, instead, to be largely an accumulation of much of the misinformation, half-truths and insinuations that for years have been directed against Japanese Americans by people with racial and economic prejudices—the same people who have been among the foremost advocates of the evacuation. A military judgment based upon such racial and sociological considerations is not entitled to the great weight ordinarily given the judgments based upon strictly military considerations. Especially is this so when every charge relative to race, religion, culture, geographical location, and legal and economic status has been substantially discredited by independent studies made by experts in these matters. . . .

No adequate reason is given for the failure to treat these Japanese Americans on an individual basis by holding investigations and hearings to separate the loyal from the disloyal, as was done in the case of persons of German and Italian ancestry. . . .

Moreover, there was no adequate proof that the Federal Bureau of Investigation and the military and naval intelligence services did not have the espionage and sabotage situation well in hand during this long period. Nor is there any denial of the fact that not one person of Japanese ancestry was accused or convicted of espionage or sabotage after Pearl Harbor while they were still free, a fact which is some evidence of the loyalty of the vast majority of these individuals and of the effectiveness of the established methods of combatting these evils. It seems incredible that under these circumstances it would have been impossible to hold loyalty hearings for the mere 112,000 persons involved—or at least for the 70,000 American citizens—especially when a large part of this number represented children and elderly men and women. . . .

I dissent, therefore, from this legalization of racism. Racial discrimination in any form and in any degree has no justifiable part whatever in our democratic way of life. It is unattractive in any setting but it is utterly revolting among a free people who have embraced the principles set forth in the Constitution of the United States. All residents of this nation are kin in some way by blood or culture to a foreign land. Yet they are primarily and necessarily a part of the new and distinct civilization of the United States. They must accordingly be treated at all times as the heirs of the American experiment and as entitled to all the rights and freedoms guaranteed by the Constitution.

William Dudley, ed., *The Bill of Rights: Opposing Viewpoints.* San Diego: Greenhaven Press, 1994, pp. 178–81.

Document 10: Applying the Fifth Amendment's Protections to the States

In the historic 1947 Adamson v. California *Supreme Court ruling, four of the nine justices voted for applying Fifth Amendment protections to the states through the due process clause of the Fourteenth Amendment, foreshadowing the nearly total incorporation of civil rights into due process by the Warren Court in the 1960s. Presented here are excerpts from the opinion of one of the four, Justice Hugo Black.*

The first ten amendments were proposed and adopted largely because of fear that Government might unduly interfere with prized individual liberties. The people wanted and demanded a Bill of Rights written into their Constitution. . . .

My study of the historical events that culminated in the Fourteenth Amendment, . . . persuades me that one of the chief objects that the provisions of the Amendment's first section, separately, and as a whole, were intended to accomplish was to make the Bill of Rights, applicable to the states. . . .

And I further contend that the "natural law" formula which the Court uses to reach its conclusion in this case should be abandoned as an incongruous excrescence [abnormal growth] on our Constitution. I believe that formula to be itself a violation of our Constitution, in that it subtly conveys to courts, at the expense of legislatures, ultimate power over public policies in fields where no specific provision of the Constitution limits legislative power. . . .

I cannot consider the Bill of Rights to be an outworn 18th Century "strait jacket". . . . Its provisions may be thought outdated abstractions by some. And it is true that they were designed to meet ancient evils. But they are the same kind of human evils that have emerged from century to century wherever excessive power is sought by the few at the expense of the many. In my judgment the people of no nation can lose their liberty so long as a Bill of Rights like ours survives and its basic purposes are conscientiously interpreted, enforced and respected so as to afford continuous protection against old, as well as new, devices and practices which might thwart those purposes. I fear to see the consequences of the Court's practice of substituting its own concepts of decency and fundamental justice for the language of the Bill of Rights as its point of departure in interpreting and enforcing that Bill of Rights. . . . I would follow what I believe was the original purpose of the Fourteenth Amendment—to extend to all the people of the nation the complete protection of the Bill of Rights. To hold that this Court can determine what, if any, provisions of the Bill of Rights will be enforced, and if so to what degree, is to frustrate the great design of a written Constitution.

Joel M. Gora, ed., *Due Process of Law*. Skokie, IL: National Textbook Company, 1977, p. 8.

Document 11: The Death Penalty Declared to Be Cruel and Unusual Punishment

In this excerpt from the majority ruling in the 1972 Furman v. Georgia *Supreme Court case, Justice William J. Brennan advocates that the death penalty, as administered in the United States at the time of the petition, constitutes cruel and unusual punishment because it does not comport with human dignity.*

The Cruel and Unusual Punishments Clause prohibits the infliction of uncivilized and inhuman punishments. The State, even as it punishes, must treat its members with respect for their intrinsic worth as human beings. A punishment is "cruel and unusual," therefore, if it does not comport with human dignity. . . .

The primary principle is that a punishment must not be so severe as to be degrading to the dignity of human beings. Pain, certainly, may be a factor in the judgment. The infliction of an extremely severe punishment will often entail physical suffering. . . .

More than the presence of pain, however, is comprehended in the judgment that the extreme severity of a punishment makes it degrading to the dignity of human beings. . . . The true significance of these punishments is that they treat members of the human race as nonhumans, as objects to be toyed with and discarded. They are thus inconsistent with the fundamental premise of the Clause that even the vilest criminal remains a human being possessed of common human dignity. . . .

In determining whether a punishment comports with human dignity, we are aided also by a second principle inherent in the Clause—that the State must not arbitrarily inflict a severe punishment. . . .

A third principle inherent in the Clause is that a severe punishment must not be unacceptable to contemporary society. Rejection by society, of course, is a strong indication that a severe punishment does not comport with human dignity. . . .

Legislative authorization, of course, does not establish acceptance. The acceptability of a severe punishment is measured, not by its availability, for it might become so offensive to society as never to be inflicted, but by its use.

The final principle inherent in the Clause is that a severe punishment must not be excessive. A punishment is excessive under this principle if it is unnecessary: The infliction of a severe punishment by the State cannot comport with human dignity when it is nothing more than the pointless infliction of suffering. . . .

The test, then, will ordinarily be a cumulative one: If a punishment is unusually severe, if there is a strong probability that it is inflicted arbitrarily, if it is substantially rejected by contemporary society, and if there is no reason to believe that it serves any penal purpose more effectively than some less severe punishment, then the continued infliction of that punishment violates the command of the Clause that the State may not inflict inhuman and uncivilized punishments upon those convicted of crimes. . . .

In sum, the punishment of death is inconsistent with all four principles: Death is an unusually severe and degrading punishment; there is a strong probability that it is inflicted arbitrarily; its rejection by contemporary society is virtually total; and there is no reason to believe that it serves any penal purpose more effectively than the less severe punishment of imprisonment. The function of these principles is to enable a court to determine whether a punishment comports with human dignity. Death, quite simply, does not.

Joel M. Gora, ed., *Due Process of Law*. Skokie, IL: National Textbook Company, 1977, pp. 168–69.

CHRONOLOGY

1215
England's king John signs the Magna Carta, guaranteeing his barons and their dependents certain established liberties, in the process creating Europe's first written bill of rights and the ancient forerunner of the U.S. version.

1689
Parliament, having become supreme over the monarchy, creates the English Bill of Rights.

1776
England's American colonies declare their independence, initiating the Revolutionary War; Virginia becomes the first colony to create its own bill of rights.

1787
Having won the war and created a new nation, American leaders meet in Philadelphia to draft a written constitution; in the months following the Constitutional Convention, the hottest issue in the debates over ratifying the document concern the inclusion of a written bill of rights.

1789
After heated debates of its own, Congress sends a proposed bill of rights made up of twelve constitutional amendments to the states for ratification.

1791
The states ratify ten of the twelve proposed amendments, comprising the federal Bill of Rights, making them part of the Constitution.

1798
The ruling Federalist Party pushes through the Sedition Act, making it a crime to criticize the government and marking the first major challenge to the First Amendment.

1863
President Abraham Lincoln defends his policy of restricting the civil rights of Northern "Confederate sympathizers" during the Civil War as being justified by national security concerns.

1866
The Supreme Court declares that Lincoln's wartime restrictions of liberties violated the Bill of Rights.

1868
Congress passes the Fourteenth Amendment to the Constitution, containing a "due process" clause similar to that in the Fifth Amendment but this time applying to the states rather than the federal government.

1918
Congress passes another Sedition Act, in this case to deal with domestic opponents of World War I.

1919
The Supreme Court upholds the conviction of Charles Schenck for conspiring to obstruct the U.S. armed forces, a ruling some say abridges freedom of speech; in a separate case, the Court finds that the Sedition Act is constitutional.

1942
Fearing they will aid the enemy during World War II, the government orders Japanese Americans evacuated from their homes and resettled in detention camps, in the process suppressing many of their civil rights.

1944
In *Korematsu v. United States*, the Supreme Court upholds the internment of Japanese Americans and the suppression of their liberties.

1947
A Louisiana man sentenced to die in the electric chair survives the attempted execution and afterward petitions the Supreme Court to exempt him from a second attempt on the grounds that it would be cruel and unusual punishment; the Court denies the petition.

1951
The Supreme Court upholds the conviction of eleven Communist Party leaders for advocating the overthrow of the U.S. government.

1957
In *Roth v. United States*, the Supreme Court upholds the conviction of a smut shop owner for mailing obscene circulars, sparking debate

about the right of the government to decide what citizens can and cannot see.

1961–1969
The Warren Court (named after Chief Justice Earl Warren) incorporates most of the guarantees of the Bill of Rights into the due process clauses of the Fifth and Fourteenth Amendments.

1972
In *Furman v. Georgia*, the Supreme Court rules that the death penalty, as administered in the United States, is unconstitutional; the states put all pending executions on hold.

1976
Expressing its satisfaction that the states, after overhauling their capital punishment procedures, can now fairly impose them, the Supreme Court reverses itself and in effect declares the death penalty constitutional.

1988
Congress passes into law the recommendations of the Commission on Wartime Relocation and Internment of Civilians, providing an official apology and monetary reparations to Japanese Americans interned during World War II.

Study Questions

Chapter 1

1. Contrast the view expressed by Brutus in Viewpoint 1—that the bills of rights formulated by the states may not provide enough security against a strong central government—with that of Edmund Randolph in Viewpoint 2, that the Constitution already sufficiently addresses civil rights concerns.

2. In Viewpoint 1, Thomas Jefferson states that a bill of rights would become a powerful weapon in the hands of the Supreme Court. How has this prediction come true? Cite two cases discussed in later chapters, in each case explaining the background and how the high court ruled.

3. What was Alexander Hamilton's reasoning in Viewpoint 2 that a bill of rights might be dangerous?

Chapter 2

1. Do you agree with Justice Holmes's formulation of the "clear and present danger" doctrine, as summarized in Viewpoints 1 and 2? Why or why not?

2. How does Justice Vinson define the "ultimate value of any society" in Viewpoint 2? Is his argument still applicable to today's United States, which has become by far the most powerful nation on earth?

3. Do you agree with the view expressed by Monsignor Howard and Sidney Callahan, that violent and degrading images can inspire antisocial behavior? Why or why not? Cite some examples from your own experience that support your argument.

4. Contrast Justice Brennan's argument in Viewpoint 3, that obscenity is not protected by the First Amendment, with that of Justice Douglas in Viewpoint 4, that censorship curtails freedom of speech.

5. Summarize the minority opinion in *Roth v. United States*, as cited in Viewpoint 4.

Chapter 3

1. Explain the relationship between the Fifth and Fourteenth Amendments, as discussed in the 1884 *Hurtado v. California* and 1947 *Adamson v. California* cases.

2. Cite at least four of the accomplishments of the Warren Court in the 1960s. Do you agree with those who say the Court went too far and hampered the efforts of law enforcement authorities? Why or why not?

3. In your judgment, is Professor Wolfe's analysis of the Fifth Amendment in Viewpoint 2 valid? Why or why not?

4. Explain what Justice Matthews meant when he defined due process as "the law of the land."

Chapter 4

1. Do you agree with Viewpoint 1, that those who say the death penalty is cruel are "out of touch with the feelings of most of their neighbors"? Why or why not?

2. Contrast Justice Burger's opinion in *Furman v. Georgia* with that of Justice Marshall in the same case.

3. What reasons does William Reynolds give in Viewpoint 1 that societal retribution is justifiable and appropriate?

4. Explain how the government's detention of Northern "Confederate sympathizers" during the Civil War was similar to its evacuation of Japanese Americans during World War II.

5. Do you agree with Justice Murphy's assessment that the Japanese internment was a case of prejudice and hysteria? Why or why not?

FOR FURTHER READING

Herbert M. Atherton and J. Jackson Barlow, eds., *1791–1991: The Bill of Rights and Beyond*. Washington, DC: Commission on the Bicentennial of the United States Constitution, 1990. This very handsomely mounted book, which is available in most schools and libraries, features many stunning photos and drawings that perfectly highlight the readable text summarizing the impact of the original ten amendments to the Constitution.

William Dudley, ed., *The Bill of Rights: Opposing Viewpoints*. San Diego: Greenhaven Press, 1994. A very well-constructed and useful volume that presents essays by various noted scholars about the meaning and impact of the Bill of Rights in American society. Each position taken is balanced by an opposing view; for example, one essay argues that mandatory flag salutes are constitutional, while another counters that such salutes violate the First Amendment.

————, ed., *The Creation of the Constitution: Opposing Viewpoints*. San Diego: Greenhaven Press, 1995. This excellent, fact-filled book presents original essays by the founding fathers in which they argue about the need for a constitution, what it should include, and how it might impact the new country. Among these are essays dealing with the Bill of Rights. The book also contains original documents, including the Articles of Confederation and, of course, the Constitution. Highly recommended.

J. Edward Evans, *Freedom of Speech*. Minneapolis: Lerner Publications, 1990. A general examination of the meaning and impact of the First Amendment in the United States. Aimed at junior high and high school readers.

Henry Mayer, *Son of Thunder*. New York: Watts, 1986. An absorbing biography of Patrick Henry, revolutionary orator, Anti-Federalist, and fighter for civil liberties. Advanced reading for young people.

Don Nardo, *The Importance of Thomas Jefferson*. San Diego: Lucent Books, 1993. A concise biography of Jefferson, including his role in the formation of the U.S. government. Useful for reports and research papers.

————, *Democracy*. San Diego: Lucent Books, 1994. This book, which can be used as a companion volume to this one on the Bill

117

of Rights, traces the origins and development of democratic thought and practice, from ancient Athens and the Roman Republic, through the Magna Carta; the development of the English Parliament; the English Bill of Rights; the ideas of Locke, Rousseau, Montesquieu, Mills, and other advocates of human rights; the American Revolution and establishment of the U.S. Constitution; the French Revolution; and the spread of democracy in the modern world.

Jerry Stanley, *I Am an American: A True Story of Japanese Internment.* New York: Crown Publishers, 1994. A well-written, informative, and moving account of the "evacuation" of Japanese Americans from the West Coast in 1942 because the government feared some of them might be disloyal. Highly recommended.

R. Conrad Stein, *The Bill of Rights.* Chicago: Childrens Press, 1992. A brief synopsis of the Bill of Rights and how it has affected American society over the years. Written for basic readers.

MAJOR WORKS CONSULTED

Raymond Arsenault, ed., *Crucible of Liberty: Two Hundred Years of the Bill of Rights*. New York: Free Press, 1991. In this collection of essays, noted scholars examine how the Bill of Rights has evolved over the course of American history.

Fred Barbash, *The Founding: A Dramatic Account of the Writing of the Constitution*. New York: Simon and Schuster, 1987. A well-written narrative of the Constitutional Convention and its major players, concluding with the private and public debate over the Bill of Rights.

Lucius J. Barker and Twiley W. Barker Jr., eds., *Civil Liberties and the Constitution: Cases and Commentaries*. Englewood Cliffs, NJ: Prentice-Hall, 1975. A collection of court cases concerning religious liberty, freedom of expression, self-incrimination, discrimination and civil rights, and other issues connected with the Bill of Rights, including some useful commentary by the editors.

David J. Bodenhamer, *Fair Trial: Rights of the Accused in American History*. New York: Oxford University Press, 1992. An excellent, readable history of the evolution of American civil rights, discussing all of the relevant Supreme Court cases.

David J. Bodenhamer and James W. Ely Jr., eds., *The Bill of Rights in Modern America After 200 Years*. Bloomington: Indiana University Press, 1993. A collection of essays by noted scholars concerning such modern Bill of Rights issues as the right to bear arms, cruel and unusual punishment, and police practices and the law.

Catherine D. Bowen, *Miracle at Philadelphia: The Story of the Constitutional Convention, May to September 1787*. Boston: Little, Brown, 1966. Of the numerous general accounts of the writing of the Constitution, this is one of the most readable and informative.

Bill F. Chamberlin and Charlene J. Brown, *The First Amendment Reconsidered: New Perspectives on the Meaning of Freedom of Speech and Press*. New York: Longman, 1982. A collection of scholarly essays focusing on the meaning of freedom of the press in the twentieth century and application of the First Amendment in the 1980s.

Gilbert Chinard, *Thomas Jefferson: The Apostle of Americanism*. Ann Arbor: University of Michigan Press, 1966. This scholarly work emphasizes Jefferson's contributions to the formation of American and democratic thought and values.

William O. Douglas, *The Right of the People*. Garden City, NY: Doubleday, 1958. The famous Supreme Court justice speaks out on important rights issues, including the conflict between free expression and community values, censorship, privacy, loyalty investigations, religious freedom, imposition of martial law, and others.

Edward Dumbauld, *The Bill of Rights and What It Means Today*. Westport, CT: Greenwood Press, 1979. This extremely informative volume begins with a detailed account of the debates over and adoption of the Bill of Rights by the founding fathers, then discusses twentieth-century judicial interpretations of the first ten amendments. Also features appendices containing numerous original documents pertaining to the Bill of Rights.

Joel M. Gora, ed., *Due Process of Law*. Skokie, IL: National Textbook Company, 1977. This very useful book contains abridgments of the major Supreme Court cases pertaining to due process (as cited in the Fifth and Fourteenth Amendments), along with concise, informative commentary on each.

Harold H. Hart, ed., *Censorship: For and Against*. New York: Hart Publishing, 1971. A somewhat dated but still relevant collection of essays by noted Americans, either supporting or denouncing the imposition of certain kinds of censorship.

Eugene W. Hickok Jr., ed., *The Bill of Rights: Original Meaning and Current Understanding*. Charlottesville: University Press of Virginia, 1991. A collection of scholarly essays examining the original intent of the Bill of Rights and how that intent has been interpreted in later cases.

Peter Iron, *The Courage of Their Convictions*. New York: Free Press, 1988. The stories of sixteen citizens who took their civil liberties cases to the Supreme Court.

Adrienne Koch and William Peden, eds., *The Life and Selected Writings of Thomas Jefferson*. New York: Random House, 1944. A very useful book for scholars, students, and anyone interested in Jefferson and/or the formative years of the United States; contains many of Jefferson's more important writings, including his letters to James Madison concerning the creation of the Bill of Rights.

Milton R. Konvitz, ed., *Bill of Rights Reader: Leading Constitutional Cases*. Ithaca, NY: Cornell University Press, 1960. A large and very useful compendium of majority and minority opinions in important Supreme Court cases pertaining to civil rights.

Forrest McDonald, *Alexander Hamilton: A Biography*. New York: Norton, 1979. An informative volume about the staunch Federalist who believed that a bill of rights was unnecessary.

Eric Neisser, *Recapturing the Spirit: Essays on the Bill of Rights at 200*. Madison, WI: Madison House, 1991. Neisser, of Rutgers Law School and the ACLU, here comments on a wide range of rights issues, including changing definitions of free speech, the right to privacy, affirmative action, homelessness, racism and the death penalty, and school prayer.

J.R. Pole, ed., *The American Constitution, For and Against: The Federalist and Anti-Federalist Papers*. New York: Hill and Wang, 1987. In this collection of original documents, the *Federalist Papers* of Jay, Hamilton, and Madison are balanced by essays by Anti-Federalists, including Brutus, Agrippa, Melancton Smith, Patrick Henry, and George Mason.

Robert Rutland, *James Madison: Founding Father*. New York: Macmillan, 1987. A well-written biography of the man often referred to as the "father" of the Bill of Rights.

Byron L. Stay, ed., *Censorship: Opposing Viewpoints*. San Diego: Greenhaven Press, 1997. A comprehensive and up-to-date collection of articles and essays about censorship, including issues such as sexually harrassing speech, government funding for the arts, book banning, pornography on the Internet, and the television V-Chip.

Herbert J. Storing, *What the Anti-Federalists Were For*. Chicago: University of Chicago Press, 1981. Examines those founding fathers (including George Mason) who opposed the Constitution as it had been drafted in the 1787 convention and their objections, particularly the lack of a written bill of rights.

Helen E. Veit et al., eds., *Creating the Bill of Rights: The Documentary Record from the First Federal Congress*. Baltimore: Johns Hopkins University Press, 1991. This extremely useful informational source includes the minutes of the meetings of the House of

Representatives from May through August of 1789, in which the Bill of Rights was debated, and also letters and other relevant documents from March through October of that same year.

Andrew D. Weinberger, *Freedom and Protection: The Bill of Rights*. San Francisco: Chandler Publishing, 1962. A useful, well-organized synopsis and commentary of important Supreme Court cases pertaining to the Bill of Rights, with some excerpts from selected high court opinions.

ADDITIONAL WORKS CONSULTED

Amnesty International, *When the State Kills . . . The Death Penalty: A Human Rights Issue*. New York: Amnesty International, 1989.

Roy P. Basler, ed., *Abraham Lincoln: His Speeches and Writings*. Cleveland: World Publishing, 1946.

Catherine D. Bowen, *John Adams and the American Revolution*. Boston: Little, Brown, 1950.

Milton C. Cummings Jr. and David Wise, *Democracy Under Pressure: An Introduction to the American Political Tradition*. New York: Harcourt Brace Jovanovich, 1974.

Daniel S. Davis, *Behind the Barbed Wire: The Imprisonment of Japanese Americans During World War II*. New York: E.P. Dutton, 1982.

William O. Douglas, *The Court Years, 1939–1975*. New York: Random House, 1980.

Ian Gray and Moira Stanley, eds., *A Punishment in Search of a Crime: Americans Speak Out Against the Death Penalty*. New York: Avon Books, 1989.

Marjorie Heins, *Sex, Sin, and Blasphemy: A Guide to America's Censorship Wars*. New York: New Press, 1993.

Alfred H. Kelly et al., *The American Constitution: Its Origins and Development*. New York: Norton, 1991.

Michael J. Lacey and Knud Haakonssen, eds., *A Culture of Rights: The Bill of Rights in Philosophy, Politics, and Law—1791–1991*. New York: Cambridge University Press, 1991.

Milton Lomask, *The Spirit of 1787: The Making of Our Constitution*. New York: Ballantine Books, 1980.

Alexander Meiklejohn, *Free Speech and Its Relation to Self-Government*. New York: Harper and Brothers, 1948.

Samuel Eliot Morison, *The Oxford History of the American People*. New York: Oxford University Press, 1965.

Don Nardo, *The Death Penalty*. San Diego: Lucent Books, 1992.

Saul K. Padover, ed., *Sources of Democracy: Voices of Freedom, Hope and Justice*. New York: McGraw-Hill, 1973.

Diane Ravitch and Abigail Thernstrom, eds., *The Democracy Reader*. New York: HarperCollins, 1992.

Robert Rutland, ed., *The Papers of George Mason, 1725–1792* (in three volumes). Chapel Hill: University of North Carolina Press, 1970.

Page Smith, *Democracy on Trial: The Japanese American Evacuation and Relocation in World War II*. New York: Simon and Schuster, 1995.

Geoffrey Stone et al., eds., *The Bill of Rights in the Modern State*. Chicago: University of Chicago Press, 1992.

Joseph Story, *Commentaries on the Constitution of the United States*. Boston: Hilliard, Gray, 1833.

Harold C. Syrett, ed., *The Papers of Alexander Hamilton, Volume IV: January 1787–May 1788*. New York: Columbia University Press, 1962.

Eugen Weber, ed., *The Western Tradition: From the Ancient World to Louis XIV*. Boston: D.C. Heath, 1965.

Carol Wekesser, ed., *The Death Penalty: Opposing Viewpoints*. San Diego: Greenhaven Press, 1991.

William H. Young, *Essentials of American Government*. New York: Appleton-Century-Crofts, 1964.

INDEX

ABOUT THE AUTHOR

Historian and award-winning author Don Nardo has written many books for young adults about American history and government, including *The U.S. Presidency, The U.S. Congress, Democracy, The War of 1812, The Mexican-American War,* and *Franklin D. Roosevelt: U.S. President.* Mr. Nardo has also written several teleplays and screenplays, including work for Warner Brothers and ABC-Television. He lives with his wife, Christine, and dog, Bud, on Cape Cod, Massachusetts.